BARBARA JORDAN

BOOK FIFTEEN / Louann Atkins Temple Women & Culture Series /
Books about women and families, and their changing role in society

BARBARA JORDAN

Speaking the Truth with Eloquent Thunder

EDITED BY MAX SHERMAN

University of Texas Press ❦ *Austin*

The Louann Atkins Temple Women & Culture Series is supported by
Allison, Doug, Taylor, and Andy Bacon; Margaret, Lawrence, Will, John,
and Annie Temple; Larry Temple; the Temple-Inland Foundation; and
the National Endowment for the Humanities.

LIBRARY OF CONGRESS CATALOGING-IN-PUBLICATION DATA

Jordan, Barbara, 1936–1996.
    Barbara Jordan / Speaking the truth with eloquent thunder ; edited
by Max Sherman. — 1st ed.
        p.   cm. — (Louann Atkins Temple women & culture series ; bk. 15)
    ISBN 978-0-292-71637-7 (cloth : alk. paper)
        1. United States—Politics and government—1974–1977. 2. United
States—Politics and government—1977–1981. 3. United States—Politics
and government—1981–1989. 4. United States—Politics and government—1989– 5. Civil rights—United States. 6. Political ethics—United
States. 7. Democracy—United States. 8. Jordan, Barbara, 1936–1996.
9. Speeches, addresses, etc., American. I. Sherman, Max R. II. Title.
III. Series.
    E838.5.J6735   2007
    328.73092—dc22
    [B]   2006017267

For the students of Barbara Jordan

Photo courtesy of the LBJ School of Public Affairs, University of Texas at Austin.

Liberty lies in the hearts of men and women; when it dies there, no constitution, no law, no court can save it; no constitution, no law, no court can even do much to help it. While it lies there it needs no constitution, no law, no court to save it . . . .

The spirit of liberty is the spirit which is not too sure that it is right; the spirit of liberty is the spirit which seeks to understand the minds of other men and women; the spirit of liberty is the spirit which weighs their interests alongside its own without bias; the spirit of liberty remembers that not even a sparrow falls to earth unheeded; the spirit of liberty is the spirit of Him who, near two thousand years ago, taught mankind that lesson it has never learned, but has never quite forgotten; that there may be a kingdom where the least shall be heard and considered side by side with the greatest . . . .

—JUDGE LEARNED HAND, MAY 21, 1944

CONTENTS

PREFACE

This book is not about "Who was Barbara Jordan?" but rather "Who *is* Barbara Jordan?" and what does she have to say to us in the twenty-first century?"

Barbara Jordan was my friend and colleague for twenty-five years. We served together in the Texas Senate and worked together for thirteen years at the Lyndon B. Johnson School of Public Affairs at the University of Texas at Austin. Barbara died on January 17, 1996, and is buried in the Texas State Cemetery in Austin, Texas.

At a motel in Colorado Springs, Colorado, on the morning of August 1, 2004, while on a drive from Texas to Montana, I awoke with a clear sense of a message from Barbara Jordan: *Max, you have read my speeches. You teach my course on "Ethics and Political Values." You have spoken on my behalf many times. You are completing our book based on the ethics course. In the election seasons of this new century, I have something to say. Get off your duff and help me say it.*

Years before, on the floor of the Texas Senate, Senator Barbara Jordan was quietly explaining a bill. I sat only two seats behind her but could not hear her. Without going through the presiding officer, I spoke directly to her, "Barbara, I can't hear you." With that magnificent voice that many of us called "the Voice of God," she looked me squarely in the eye and said emphatically, "Max, you'll hear me when I want you to hear me."

Time ran out for the 2004 elections, but in this 2008 election season, Barbara wants all who will to listen and to hear her.

And Barbara also wants to do some preaching.

At her funeral in the sanctuary of Good Hope Missionary Baptist Church in Houston, her pastor, D. Z. Cofield, presided. Knowing that he was speaking to a national television audience and to a congregation that included the president of the United States, members of the cabinet and other federal officers, the former governor of Texas, the mayor of Houston, and other dignitaries, Pastor Cofield asked, "What should I say to this distinguished gathering?" He pointed to the right back corner of the church where Barbara used to sit and said, "If Sister Barbara were here and I asked her that question, she would say, 'Preach, Pastor, preach.'" And preach he did.

My hope and my prayer is that this little book of Barbara's own words will preach to a nation at this important time in history.

MAX SHERMAN
Professor Emeritus and former Dean
Lyndon B. Johnson School of Public Affairs (1983–1997)
Austin, Texas
September 2006

Powerful preaching and enthusiastic hymn singing were important to Barbara Jordan. Any proceeds from this little book will go to the Center for Proclamation and Worship and the Chair for Sacred Music at the Austin Presbyterian Theological Seminary.

ACKNOWLEDGMENTS

I owe thanks to many: to students in my class on "Ethics and Political Values" at the Lyndon B. Johnson School of Public Affairs who heard stories and references to Barbara Jordan and knew that Barbara, Paul Burka (my co-teacher), and I had planned to produce an anthology for the teaching of ethics based on the courses we had taught and who, after Barbara's death, challenged me to complete a book in honor of her; to Shinjini Kumar, our research assistant for the anthology, who located many materials that were resources for this book; to Martha Harrison for encouraging me and for locating material that was often difficult to find; to Mike Gillette for locating Jordan's message to the National Prayer Breakfast; to Dagmar Hamilton, Nancy Earl, Diana Wienbroer, Marilyn Duncan, and various anonymous readers for reading versions of the book and for their helpful comments; to Stephen Littrell for sharing his considerable research skills; to Marvin Wofford for inviting me to speak to the Wimberley Democrats on the subject "What Would Barbara Jordan Do?"; to Joanna Hitchcock and Bill Bishel for sharing the vision of a small book on Barbara Jordan; and to the LBJ School for providing so many opportunities to work with Barbara Jordan. And to Gene Alice Sherman, for encouragement and support, and for being my partner in this and every endeavor.

BARBARA JORDAN

Jordan at her desk during her first term in the Texas Senate. Photo courtesy of Barbara Jordan Archives, Robert James Terry Library, Texas Southern University, Houston.

BIOGRAPHY OF BARBARA C. JORDAN
(1936–1996)

Barbara Jordan's distinguished public service career began with her election to the Texas Legislature in 1966. Jordan's victory made her the first African American woman to serve in the Texas Senate and the first African American elected to that body since 1883. In 1972 she became the first African American woman from the South to be elected to the United States Congress, serving as a member of the House of Representatives until 1979.

The highlights of Jordan's legislative career include her landmark speech during Richard Nixon's impeachment hearings in 1974, her successful efforts in 1975 to expand the Voting Rights Act to include language minorities, and her keynote address to the Democratic National Convention in 1976.

From 1979 until her death in 1996, Jordan served as a distinguished professor at the Lyndon B. Johnson School of Public Affairs at the University of Texas at Austin, holding the Lyndon B. Johnson Centennial Chair in National Policy. Her students knew her as a rigorous mentor and a dedicated professor. The word "teacher" is part of her epitaph and serves as a potent reminder of her commitment to what she considered the most important role of her lifetime.

The list of accolades bestowed upon Barbara Jordan is rich and varied. She was the recipient of thirty-one honorary doctorates and numerous national awards. In 1994 President Bill Clinton presented her with the Presidential Medal of Freedom, and in 1999 *Texas Monthly* magazine named her "Role Model of the Century."

Jordan was born February 21, 1936, in Houston, one of three daughters of a Baptist preacher and warehouse clerk. She attended public schools and graduated from Texas Southern University, where she majored in political science. She received her law degree in 1959 from Boston University.[1]

STUDENT COMMENTS

These statements reflect Barbara Jordan's continuing influence on her students' lives:

- Professor Jordan makes you look at your soul.

- She has a driving concern about the world. She cares about it, and she wants us to go out there and make a difference in a positive way.

- Her ideas of social commitment and social consciousness have framed my life. She is convincing us that we have to, in a sense, pay rent for the space that we occupy.

- I've never met a person who believed so strongly that we can actually change the world. That gives me confidence that we really can.

- Above all else, she has taught me that greatness, more than power or fame, is something you do every day.

When you listen to their comments, you know that you are hearing something fundamental about leadership, about education, about public service, and about the relationship between a teacher and her students.

Making a point during the Summer Minority Advancement Program at UT Austin's LBJ School of Public Affairs. Photo by María de la Luz Martínez, courtesy of the LBJ School of Public Affairs, University of Texas at Austin.

Jordan during an interview with *Family Circle* magazine, October 10, 1976. In the background is Lady Bird Johnson. LBJ Library photo by Frank Wolf, courtesy of the Lyndon B. Johnson Presidential Library, Austin.

Congresswoman Barbara Jordan in her Washington office. Photo courtesy of Barbara Jordan Archives, Robert James Terry Library, Texas Southern University, Houston.

MY PERSONAL INTRODUCTION
OF BARBARA JORDAN

I take my cue from Henry Steele Commager, one of the nation's most distinguished historians and teachers, who died in March 1998. This consummate teacher said, "What every college must do is hold up before the young the spectacle of greatness" in history, literature, and life. I would go a step further and say that all of us in public service must hold up before the young—and the public—the spectacle of greatness.

How will we do this? If I have a theme, it centers on the life of Barbara Jordan, who was my friend and colleague for twenty-five years. For most people in public life, she symbolized what ethics and values are.

In 1988 Barbara almost drowned. I was at my mother's home in the Texas Panhandle when the call came informing me of the accident. I immediately boarded a plane and came to Austin. I went from the airport to the hospital. The intensive care area was closed, but being a politician, and in my youth a door-to-door Bible salesman, I found an open door and a friendly custodian who took me through the maze of hallways to her room. Her attending physician was still there. I identified myself and he let me stay. They were not sure she would live through the night. I held her hand, but because she was unconscious, she did not know I was there.

Later, while still in the hospital and unsure of her future, Barbara invited a few people to come and spend some time with her. We did not talk about politics or policy matters, but fundamental, basic values. We even worked in a little religion.

Barbara lived for eight additional years. That near miss with death shaped the rest of her life. I am convinced that she approached her teaching, her life, and her commentary on important public events with a new intensity. She had renewed her commitment to higher moral values.

In the administration of Governor Ann Richards of Texas, Barbara Jordan served as the "Ethics Czar." She addressed and charged every new group of gubernatorial appointees on matters of ethics. One of those appointees remembers that Barbara also scared them to death by telling them that they were now "public servants" and that there is a vast difference between "public" and "private." Barbara's message was this: you will make more money in the private sector; you can conduct most of your business in secret; you do not have to tell others how you spend your money. Private activity is more efficient; there are not as many rules and regulations. In public life you will not get rich; your business will be conducted in the open; your budgets will be open to the public; it is terribly inefficient because of the many rules and regulations to ensure public accountability.

She told those public servants and all of her students that public service is the price we pay for the space we occupy on this earth. It is the highest calling. One does not enter it lightly.

I was fortunate to have a choice seat at Barbara's funeral at the Good Hope Missionary Baptist Church in Houston. Luminaries and dignitaries from throughout the nation were there, as well as lines upon lines of average, ordinary people who had come to pay their respects. A nation was holding up "the spectacle of greatness" for the young and for the whole world to see.

Even now, some of the following events strike me as uncanny, even eerie.

At Christmastime in 1995, Barbara was hospitalized again. I went unannounced to her room, as I always did (because if you called ahead, the answer from hospitals, doctors, or attendants was always "no"). She was in intensive care, this time at another Austin hospital. The nurse told her I was there, and I was invited in. She was not well. While I was there, her doctor came to report some test results. I offered to leave, but she asked me to stay and asked the doctor to go ahead. It was not good news. Medically, Barbara was not given long to live. By her choice, she went home and had excellent care.

On a Tuesday morning, January 16, 1996, I went to my office, but an instinct told me to drive down to Manchaca, a few miles south of Austin, to see Barbara. Unannounced, I knocked on the door. I was invited in. The breathing machine was not working, and two nurses were trying to make it work. Two of Barbara's close friends asked me to come into another room to talk. They confided that Barbara "never thought she would die" and, consequently, had not made specific plans for her death. I left there with three tasks: to contact Bill Moyers to see if he would speak at a memorial service, to contact her lawyer and tell him Barbara was dying, and to see if a burial place could be arranged in the Texas State Cemetery.

By noon the first two tasks were completed and the third was on track. I had an appointment to meet the superintendent of the State Cemetery the next afternoon. All of us were going to meet at the lawyer's office the next morning at ten. Before we met for those appointments, just before 9:30 the next morning, Barbara's close friend called to tell me, "It's over." Barbara had just died, January 17, 1996.

We did meet later that morning. Stan, a longtime friend of Barbara's, and I were dispatched to pick a plot in the State Cemetery. The cemetery's superintendent had worked in the State Senate when Barbara and I served there. He called me "Senator Sherman" and called Barbara "Senator Jordan." He told us that because of recent renovations the old, original hill had three possible places. He picked out what he thought was the "choice" plot. The geography was perfect, but knowing Barbara's politics, we felt that the company of very conservative Texas politicians was problematic. Stan and I agreed we should look at the "second best" spot.

I should add that earlier I had asked Barbara's closest friend what we were looking for. She jokingly said, "Well, you know Barbara. It needs to be on the highest hill, and next to Stephen F. Austin [known as the 'Father of Texas']." I laughed with her, knowing that is what Barbara would have wanted, but now it appeared impossible.

Stan and I went to the spot on the back side of the hill, measured it, and looked over the adjoining graves. Stan said, "I think this is it." It was on the old hill. But I had the nagging feeling that we should see the last spot, which was considered unworkable. It had been reserved for Col. James W. Fannin, one of the early Texas heroes who was buried at Goliad. Fannin's daughter was already buried close by. But the proposed renovation plans of the State Cemetery included a separate area for "Texas Heroes."[2] So, for the first time in more than one hundred years, this spot was available. The superintendent said, "It may not have enough space, since it was designed for little people of another era, and Senator Jordan was a big woman." I asked him to measure it anyway. "Lo and behold, Senator, it will work," he said. And that is where she was buried. Barbara's grave is at the top of the highest hill in the Texas State Cemetery, and it corners on the grave of Stephen F. Austin!

What does all of this have to do with ethics for those of us living and meeting tough challenges today?

Barbara Jordan distilled ethics down to its essence. But how? Where did this innate sense of right and wrong, of "oughtness," come from? I think it came out of her upbringing in a Baptist minister's manse, out of her education, out of her dogged determination against gender and racial barriers, out of her overcoming the frailties of the human body, out of her success as an elected public servant and her preeminence as a teacher.

This is what Barbara said in an interview given shortly before her death. It is a surprisingly simple definition:

Ethical behavior means being honest, telling the truth, and doing what you said you would do.

At an earlier, happier time, there was an all-day picnic at Barbara's riverside home to celebrate her first ten years of teaching and preparing graduate students for public service. Her students came back from Washington, D.C., and many other places across this country and abroad. One of those students, who returned to Texas for the first time in ten years in order to attend the event, said this about Professor Jordan: "Above all else, she has taught me that greatness, more than power or fame, is something you do every day."

By holding up Barbara Jordan as a "spectacle of greatness," those of us who call ourselves "public servants" take on the mantle of telling the truth, whether we be president, special counsel, judge, elected or appointed official, public employee; we are honest; we tell the truth; we protect and care for the public and public resources; and we do what we said we would do when we accepted our respective public service positions.

If we call ourselves "public servants," we should live our lives in such a way that whenever we retire, or are honored or recognized by our agency or college or public institution, or just whenever we are remembered by our colleagues, we are remembered for living and conducting our public business in the most honorable, ethical way.

Few of us will have the opportunity to be on the nation's center stage as Barbara Jordan was, but each of us should aspire to be remembered as a "spectacle of greatness" in our own small corner of this planet. Even if we cannot change the world, the state, or even our agency, we can, to borrow from Mahatma Gandhi, influence our own "zone of peace." This should be our goal.

EROSION OF CIVIL LIBERTIES

MY ONE REGRET FOR THIS SMALL BOOK ON THE WORDS AND wisdom of Barbara Jordan is that her May 11, 1974, commencement address at Howard University, "Erosion of Civil Liberties," was not recorded in her own voice. It should be the first speech on the DVD that accompanies this text. It *is* the first speech in the book because she warns us about the mortal danger of entering into a Faustian bargain to give up a little liberty to obtain a little safety. As a fifteen-year-old boy making my first trip to the Statue of Liberty, I made a note from a plaque in the statue's narrow, winding staircase. My note was this quotation from Benjamin Franklin: "They that can give up essential liberty to obtain a little safety deserve neither liberty nor safety." Barbara's 1974 warning was that we not make this bargain "under the guise of the maintenance of national security."

Barbara's emphatic statement that "your government has violated civil liberties" was supported by early 1970s examples of the expansion of government power to use wiretaps, search warrants, and other surveillance techniques—examples familiar to us now through the USA Patriot Act. She then addressed the consequences for those graduates to whom she was speaking:

> You, the graduate, will emerge from academia with the expectation, and with the hope, that you will be free to pursue your life as you define it, and you are going to hope that no one will interfere with your definition of your life. You have a basis for that presumption because there is something in the history of the United States which says that freedom, that liberty, is a part of what we are about. That history started in 1776, and now, almost two hundred years later, those freedoms which were so painfully gained

are threatened by erosion. That threat has become so serious that one can ask the question as to whether "civil liberties" is any longer an operative ideal in the United States of America.

She later adds this stark assessment: "The events of the past few years and even the past few days have convinced us that it is possible for this country to stand on the edge of repression and tyranny and never know it."

It is important to remember that these words of warning were delivered to new college graduates just two months before thirty-eight-year-old Congresswoman Barbara Jordan stepped onto the world's stage as she delivered her testimony before the House Judiciary Committee on the impeachment of a president of the United States, July 25, 1974.

The text of Barbara Jordan's remarks is from the transcription filed in the Moorland-Spingarn Research Center at Howard University. I am grateful to Clifford L. Muse, Jr., for locating this refreshing speech. It sounds like Barbara Jordan. Even though there is no audio of her speech, some might think Barbara had come back from her grave at the State Cemetery in Austin, Texas, to give this warning about many of the provisions of the Patriot Act and the current plague of secrecy in government.

If you read only one of Barbara Jordan's speeches, read this one. It is a *must read.*

Congresswoman Barbara Jordan being sworn in by Speaker of the House
Carl Albert, January 1973. Photo courtesy of Barbara Jordan Archives,
Robert James Terry Library, Texas Southern University, Houston.

Thank you very much. Thank you very much. To Dr. Cheek, or should I say "Little Caesar," to the distinguished graduates here, I am quite pleased that you asked me to say some words on the occasion of this graduation. What I have said in the past has been called many things, but it's never been called the Convocation Oration, and so that's what we have today.

I suppose in addressing you graduates I should call you "presumptive graduates." I note on the program that you are only presumed to have completed the requirements and that that presumption is inconclusive until you receive the paper, and I hope you receive it.

For those of you who feel I am going to give you an oration which is going to exhort you in the tradition of commencement addresses, suffice it to say that "you are hereby exhorted," and that is the most I'll do on that. I suppose in light of most recent events I should say for those who came to Washington to this occasion, "welcome to the national exorcism."

I am going to talk about civil liberties. Civil liberties—and if you write this subject, write *civil liberties, colon,* and then after that, write *inoperative,* and put a question mark; write *inaudible, question mark; illegible, question mark; expletive deleted, question mark.*

On the thirtieth day of April, the members of the Committee on the Judiciary received a document. That document purported to be the recorded conversations of the president of the United States. There are some omissions. One thousand six hundred seventy portions of conversations were marked either inaudible or illegible. One wonders what remains—what in the world remains—in terms of acts or in terms of deeds undiscovered because of some reason they could not be heard or could not be understood.

Is it possible—I raise the rhetorical question—that individual liberties, that civil liberties, that individual freedoms, are somehow masked behind these little words: *inoperative, inaudible, unintelligible, expletive deleted;* if you answer those questions in the affirmative I would say that there is some justification for doing that in light of past and present events. Your government has violated civil liberties. It admitted—the Government of the United States of America admitted—that it wire-tapped its own employees seventeen times. Newsmen, fearful that the First Amendment protections of freedom of the press are more rhetoric than fact, have come to the Congress and sought the passage of a Newsman's Shield Law. The politicization of the FBI has now become a matter of congressional oversight. The president's right to suspend—or alleged right to suspend—the Fourth Amendment against unreasonable searches and seizures in the national security interests is somehow defended. The concept of executive privilege has been used rather cavalierly to disguise gross intrusions into the private life of the individual. You, the graduate, will emerge from academia with the expectation, and with the hope, that you will be free to pursue your life as you define it, and you are going to hope that no one will interfere with your definition of your life. You have a basis for that presumption because there is something in the history of the United States which says that freedom, that liberty, is a part of what we are about. That history started in 1776, and now, almost two hundred years later, those freedoms which were so painfully gained are threatened by erosion: That threat has become so serious that one can ask the question as to whether "civil liberties" is any longer an operative ideal in the United States of America.

Thomas Jefferson, a great president, in his first inaugural address, talked about civil liberties, talked about freedom, talked about justice and equality when he said "equal and exact justice to all men of whatever persuasion; religious, political, peace, commerce, honest friendship with all Nations; entangling alliances with none; freedom of religion, freedom of the press; freedom of person; these are the principles," said Mr. Jefferson, which should guide the republic; and then Jefferson went on to ask the question "Would the honest patriot, in the full tide of successful experiment, abandon a Government which has so far kept us firm and kept us free?" It is the "stuff" of America that its citizens want to be free of government intrusions into their private lives and into their personal affairs. This concept of freedom in America is etched into the Constitution of the United States, into the Bill of Rights. There are no gaps; there are no inexplicable "hums" in the Constitution of the United States. The language of that document flows well. The men who sought to get it passed, who sought to get it ratified, fought for it because they felt that they were constructing a nation, the touchstone of which would be liberty and freedom and justice—they thought that—they felt that—they were building—creating—a new nation with a system of government with checks and balances and separation of powers which would forever protect the citizens of the United States from gross abuses of power by public officials and by gross excesses of power by the government of the United States. The signers of that Constitution felt that we now had a government which would secure the blessings of liberty to ourselves and our posterity. We know that that liberty is shaky because modern technology now has invested the government with the tools to invade private affairs through certain kinds of electronic mechanisms. Thomas Jefferson, again, warned us that the natural progress of things is for liberty to yield and government to gain ground—liberty to yield and government to gain ground; the natural progress of things, said Jefferson.

In recent years we have witnessed a willingness to accelerate the erosion of these guiding principles in American life. This erosion is very insidious because it didn't happen all at once, but it happened one step at a time. It happened under the guise of law and order. This erosion of civil liberties happened under the guise of the maintenance of national security; it happened, this erosion, under the guise of the legalisms of executive privilege. We know that an American president, we know that his top assistants, believed that the First and Fourth Amendments of the Constitution of the United States could be suspended. The Amendments which say that a person has a right not to be searched or to be seized unreasonably. We know that there have been attempts by the government against political opponents to somehow prevent their exercise of free speech because somehow what they had to say did not meet government approval.

The Constitution and the Bill of Rights; a balance between the interests of the government and interests of the governed. The history of individual liberty, particularly that of the right of privacy, has been a history of resistance by the people of this country to governmental encroachments upon that which we hold private.

For example, in 1603 under English Common Law, this principle was stated which became incorporated in the Fourth Amendment of the Constitution. The principle was stated this way:

> *In all cases where the King is party, the Sheriff, if the doors be not open, may break in the party's house, either to arrest him or to do other execution of the King's process, if otherwise he cannot get in, but before he breaks in [said the Law in 1603] he ought to signify the cause of his coming and make request to open the door.*

In 1766 the sanctity of the individual's right to privacy in his home was again stated with great clarity by William Pitt. The

Parliament of Great Britain was trying to impose a tax on cider, and people were resistant to paying the tax, and so the Parliament talked about passing a law that would allow the government to enter into a man's home, a man's cottage, and get the tax. This is what William Pitt said about that:

> *The poorest man, the poorest man may,* in *his cottage, bid defiance to all the forces of the Crown. It, the cottage, may be frail, the roof may shake, the wind may blow through it, the storm may enter, the rain may enter, but the King of England cannot enter. All of these forces—all of his forces dare not cross the threshold of that ruined tenement.*

Two hundred and eight years after that stirring declaration by William Pitt, what are we faced with? We are faced with state, federal, and local authorities breaking into a man's home in a mistaken frenzy because they have uncorroborated tips that he is a suspect the government needs; witness: the Collinsville, Illinois, cases.

Last summer, John Erlichman testified before the Senate Watergate Committee; Senator Talmadge, being familiar with the English Common Law principle as enunciated and affirmed by William Pitt, asked Mr. Erlichman about that principle derived from English Law—that the King of England may not enter a man's home without his consent. How did Mr. Erlichman reply? He said, "I am afraid that has been considerably eroded over the years." Eroded? Or inoperative, or inaudible, or illegible—any word you apply to it—which one is it? In addition to the continuing reality of smashed doors and actual physical invasion of private homes, we know that the government has more sophisticated and more invidious tools—electronic tools. We also know that at least fifty federal agencies have substantial investigative and enforcement functions providing a core of some 20,000 investigators, working for such agencies as: the FBI, National Intelligence, the Post Office, the Narcotics Bureau of the Justice Department, the Securities and Exchange Commission, the Internal Revenue Service, the Food and Drug Administration, the State Department, the Civil Service Commission, and even the Department of Agriculture. They've all got their little policemen.

The events of the past several years have shown us, and reveal to us, a very shocking pattern of disregard for Constitutional principles and for due process of law. It is apparent that the powerful tools of government spying and espionage against private citizens in pursuit of their lawful activities have not kept within the legitimate bounds of self-restraint and self-discipline. Justice Brandeis enunciated the principle more clearly than many when he said this: "In a government of laws, existence of the government will be imperiled if the government fails to comply with the law."

Our government is the potent, omnipresent teacher for good or for ill. It teaches the whole people by example. If the government becomes a law breaker, it breeds contempt for law and invites man to become a law in and of himself. If one thing is clear about the erosion of civil liberties, it is that there is no clear line between freedom and repression. Freedom is the fluid, intangible condition of our society. It thrives in some periods and it is beset in other periods. The events of the past few years and even the past few days have convinced us that it is possible for this country to stand on the edge of repression and tyranny and never know it. If the faith in the future is to be restored, if that which is good about the history of this country is to be regained, you must restore it; you must regain it. It would appear that this country is adrift right now; that the Ship of State is bobbing and weaving, and the words of Seneca come to mind: If a man does not know to what port he sails, no wind is favorable.

You ought to know where you are going; you ought to know to what port you sail, and perhaps the winds will favor your direction. *You* must *know* that. It is the confidence of your knowledge; it is the sureness of your knowledge which may perchance nudge this country in the right direction.

Daniel Webster said something which is etched on the walls of the United States House of Representatives, and I give it to you. He said:

> *Let us develop the resources of our land. Call forth its powers, build up its institutions, promote all its great interests, and see whether we also in our day and generation may not perform something worthy to be remembered.*

Remember how we began: *Civil Liberties, colon; Inoperative, question mark? Inaudible? Illegible? Expletive deleted?* Answer those questions in the negative. Affirm to everybody who will hear you that civil liberties are operative; that "civil liberties" *is* legible; that *no* expletive is intended and *no* expletive is necessary when you are discussing the freedoms and justice and liberty and foundation of this country. There are no brave new political worlds for you to discover out there. There are no new and innovative and creative structures for you to discover out there, but reaffirm what ought to be. Get back to the truth; that's old, but get back to it. Get back to what's honest; tell government to do that. Affirm the civil liberties of the people of this country. Do that. And I suspect that you will have performed something in your day and generation which is worthy to be remembered.

THE NATIONAL POLITICAL STAGE

RISING TO THE OCCASION

BARBARA JORDAN AND I MET AND BECAME FRIENDS IN THE Texas legislative session that began in January of 1971. As members of the Texas Senate we had twelve of thirteen identical committee assignments. My family joined Barbara and several other senate families for a retreat in East Texas that year. My son and daughter fell in love with Barbara, who treated them as individuals and helped them to join in the gospel sing-along, which she led as she played her guitar.

That session was also a precursor of events that later shaped all of our lives. One week after I was sworn into my first term as a state senator, the first indication of a major legislative scandal began to rumble through the halls of the capitol. The end result was the Sharpstown Bank Scandal, which led to several indictments and later convictions of key members of the legislature. In the next general election, in 1974, the voters elected 78 new members of the 150-member House of Representatives, 16 new members of the 31-member Texas Senate, a new governor, a new lieutenant governor, and a new attorney general. The political landscape of Texas changed dramatically.[3]

Because the 1971 legislative session followed the 1970 decennial census, the legislature was required to reapportion both its federal and state electoral districts to reflect population changes. The political stars were aligned: a safe congressional district was drawn for Barbara in the heart of Houston, and in the 1972 general election that followed she was elected with 80 percent of the total vote and 90 percent of the black vote.[4] At the same time, sitting president Richard Nixon defeated George McGovern with 61 percent of the popular vote to 38 percent. Nixon carried forty-nine states. Events surrounding this election would sculpt Barbara's congressional career.

Just as the repercussions of the Sharpstown Bank Scandal were subsiding in Texas, a trickle of rumors started flowing from the Watergate

Hotel in Washington, D.C., rumors about President Nixon's involvement in lies, cover-ups, and hidden White House tapes. Barbara Jordan was the junior member of the House Judiciary Committee charged with investigating these allegations to determine if they constituted impeachable offenses. She ranked thirty-eighth on a committee of thirty-eight members.

After months of meetings and hearings, the Judiciary Committee voted to permit prime-time television coverage of its July 24–25, 1974, sessions. Each of the thirty-eight members would have fifteen minutes to make an opening statement. Barbara Jordan was scheduled to be the third speaker on July 24.

Just before nine o'clock in the evening, the hour when most Americans were in front of their television sets, Chairman Peter Rodino called on her: "I recognize the gentlelady from Texas, Ms. Jordan, for the purpose of general debate, not to exceed a period of fifteen minutes."

For the next eleven minutes, the gentle lady from Texas held a nation spellbound as she assessed the actions of the president and explained to the American people why those actions posed a threat to the United States and the Constitution.[5]

Congresswoman Jordan's remarks on that occasion catapulted her to the center of the nation's political stage, just two and one-half months after her commencement address to the graduates of Howard University. Many of us can quote her eloquent words from the deliberations that resulted in a vote to impeach President Nixon.

> *My faith in the Constitution is whole, it is complete, it is total. I am not going to sit here and be an idle spectator to the diminution, the subversion, the destruction of the Constitution.*

Her opening remarks demonstrated how skillfully she could use her personal experience to make a point:

> *"We the People"—it is a very eloquent beginning. But when the Constitution of the United States was completed on the seventeenth of September 1787, I was not included in that "We the Peo-*

ple." I felt for many years that somehow George Washington and Alexander Hamilton just left me out by mistake. But through the process of amendment, interpretation, and court decision I have finally been included in "We the People."

Here in text and on DVD is Barbara Jordan speaking to the nation at one of the most critical moments in our history.

Jordan addressing her colleagues in the Texas Senate. Photo courtesy of Barbara Jordan Archives, Robert James Terry Library, Texas Southern University, Houston.

THE CONSTITUTIONAL BASIS FOR IMPEACHMENT, U.S. HOUSE JUDICIARY COMMITTEE IMPEACHMENT HEARINGS, WASHINGTON, D.C., JULY 25, 1974

Mr. Chairman:

I join my colleague Mr. Rangel in thanking you for giving the junior members of this committee the glorious opportunity of sharing the pain of this inquiry. Mr. Chairman, you are a strong man, and it has not been easy, but we have tried as best we can to give you as much assistance as possible.

Earlier today, we heard the beginning of the Preamble to the Constitution of the United States, "We, the People." It is a very eloquent beginning. But when that document was completed on the seventeenth of September 1787, I was not included in that "We, the People." I felt somehow for many years that George Washington and Alexander Hamilton just left me out by mistake. But through the process of amendment, interpretation, and court decision I have finally been included in "We, the People."

Today, I am an inquisitor. And hyperbole would not be fictional and would not overstate the solemnness that I feel right now. My faith in the Constitution is whole, it is complete, it is total. And I am not going to sit here and be an idle spectator to the diminution, the subversion, the destruction of the Constitution.

Who can so properly be the inquisitors for the nation as the repre-sentatives of the nation themselves. The subjects of its jurisdiction are those offenses which proceed from the misconduct of public men. And that is what we are talking about. In other words, [the jurisdiction comes] from the abuse or violation of some public trust. It is wrong, I suggest, it is a misreading of the Constitution, for any member here to assert that for a member to vote for an article of impeachment means that that member must be convinced that the president should be removed from office.

The Constitution doesn't say that. The powers relating to impeachment are an essential check in the hands of the body, the legislature, against and upon the encroachments of the executive. [In establishing] the division between the two branches of the legislature, the House and the Senate, assigning to the one the right to accuse and to the other the right to judge, the framers of this Constitution were very astute. They did not make the accusers and the judges the same person.

We know the nature of impeachment. We have been talking about it awhile now. It is chiefly designed for the president and his high ministers to somehow be called into account. It is designed to "bridle" the executive if he engages in excesses. It is designed as a method of national inquest into the conduct of public men. The framers confined in the Congress the power, if need be, to remove the president in order to strike a delicate balance between a president swollen with power and grown tyrannical and preservation of the independence of the executive. The nature of impeachment: a narrowly channeled exception to the separation-of-powers maxim; the federal convention of 1787 said that. It limited impeachment to high crimes and misdemeanors and discounted and opposed the term "maladministration." "It is to be used only for great misdemeanors," so it was said in the North Carolina ratification convention. And in the Virginia ratification convention: "We do not trust our liberty to a particular branch. We need one branch to check the others."

No one need be afraid. The North Carolina ratification convention: "No one need to be afraid that officers who commit oppression will pass with immunity." If the impeachment provisions will not reach the offenses charged here, then perhaps that eighteenth-century Constitution should be abandoned to a twentieth-century paper shredder.

"Prosecutions of impeachments will seldom fail to agitate the passions of the whole community," said Hamilton in the *Federalist Papers*, number 65. "We divide into parties more or less friendly or inimical to the accused." I do not mean political parties in that sense.

The drawing of political lines goes to the motivation behind impeachment; but impeachment must proceed within the confines of the constitutional term, "high crime and misdemeanors."

Of the impeachment process, it was Woodrow Wilson who said that "nothing short of the grossest offenses against the plain law of the land will suffice to give them speed and effectiveness. Indignation so great as to overgrow party interest may secure a conviction; but nothing else can."

Common sense would be revolted if we engaged upon this process for petty reasons. Congress has a lot to do: appropriations, tax reform, health insurance, campaign finance reform, housing, environmental protection, energy sufficiency, mass transportation. Pettiness cannot be allowed to stand in the face of such overwhelming problems. So today we are not being petty. We are trying to be *big*, because the task we have before us is a big one.

This morning, in a discussion of the evidence, we were told that the evidence which purports to support the allegations of misuse of the CIA by the president is thin. We are told that that evidence is insufficient. What that recital of the evidence this morning did not include is what the president *did* know on June 23, 1972. The president did know that it was Republican money, that it was money from the Committee for the Re-election of the President, which was found in the possession of one of the burglars arrested on June 17.

What the president did know on the twenty-third of June was the prior activities of E. Howard Hunt, which included his participation in the break-in of Daniel Ellsberg's psychiatrist; which included Howard Hunt's participation in the Dita Beard ITT affair; which included Howard Hunt's fabrication of cables designed to discredit the Kennedy Administration.

We were further cautioned today that perhaps these proceedings ought to be delayed because certainly there would be new evidence forthcoming from the President of the United States. There has not even been an obfuscated indication that this committee would receive any additional materials from the president. The committee subpoena is outstanding and if the president wants to supply that material, the committee sits here. The fact is that on yesterday, the American people waited with great anxiety for eight hours, not knowing whether their president would obey an order of the Supreme Court of the United States.

At this point, I would like to juxtapose a few of the impeachment criteria with some of the actions the president has engaged in.

Impeachment criteria: James Madison, from the Virginia ratification convention. "If the president be connected in any suspicious manner with any person and there be grounds to believe that he will shelter him, he may be impeached."

We have heard time and time again that the evidence reflects the payment to the defendants of money. The president had knowledge that these funds were being paid and these were funds collected for the 1972 presidential campaign. We know that the president met with Mr. Henry Petersen twenty-seven times to discuss matters related to Watergate, and immediately thereafter met with the very persons who were implicated in the information Mr. Petersen was receiving. The words are, "If the president be connected in any suspicious manner with any person and there be grounds to believe that he will shelter that person, he may be impeached."

Justice Story: "Impeachment is intended for occasional and extraordinary cases where a superior power acting for the whole people is put into operation to protect their rights and rescue their liberties from violations."

We know about the Houston plan. We know about the break-in of the psychiatrist's office. We know that there were absolute, complete directions on September 3 when the president instructed Ehrlichman to "do whatever is necessary." This instruction indicated that a surreptitious entry had been made in Dr. Fielding's office after [those breaking in] met with Mr. Ehrlichman and Mr. Young. "Protect their rights." "Rescue their liberties from violation."

The [South] Carolina ratification convention impeachment criteria: Those are impeachable "who behave amiss or betray their public trust."

Beginning shortly after the Watergate break-in and continuing to the present time, the president has engaged in a series of public statements and actions designed to thwart the lawful investigation by government prosecutors. Moreover, the president has made public announcements and assertions bearing on the Watergate case which the evidence will show he knew to be false. These assertions, false assertions; impeachable, those who misbehave. Those who "behave amiss or betray their public trust."

James Madison, again at the constitutional convention: "A President is impeachable if he attempts to subvert the Constitution."

The Constitution charges the president with the task of taking care that the laws be faithfully executed, and yet the president has counseled his aides to commit perjury, willfully disregard the secrecy of grand jury proceedings, conceal surreptitious entry, attempt to compromise a federal judge, while publicly displaying his cooperation with the processes of criminal justice. "A President is impeachable if he attempts to subvert the Constitution."

If the impeachment provision in the Constitution of the United States will not reach the offenses charged here, then perhaps that eighteenth-century Constitution should be abandoned to a twentieth-century paper shredder.

Has the president committed offenses and planned and directed and acquiesced in a course of conduct which the Constitution will not tolerate? That is the question. We know that. We know the question. We should now forthwith proceed to answer the question.

It is reason, and not passion, which must guide our deliberations, guide our debate, and guide our decision.

Mr. Chairman, I yield back the balance of my time.

CENTER STAGE

IN 1976 BARBARA JORDAN'S HISTORIC WORDS TO THE HOUSE Judiciary Committee were replayed to introduce her as the keynote speaker to the Democratic National Convention. The crowd in New York City's Madison Square Garden erupted with sustained shouts and applause.

She brought that raucous hall to an eerie silence before she said a word. She stood there until all was quiet, then she emphasized:

But there is something different tonight. There is something special about tonight. What is different? What is special? I, Barbara Jordan, am a keynote speaker.

After another explosion of shouts and clapping, she added:

My presence here is one additional bit of evidence that the American Dream need not forever be deferred.

She then turned subtly to politics, although it should be noted that her thirty-minute keynote speech was largely nonpartisan. The following remarks are just as applicable in 2007 as they were in 1976:

I could easily spend this time praising the accomplishments of this party and attacking the Republicans but I don't choose to do that.

I could list the many problems which Americans have. I could list the problems which cause people to feel cynical, angry, frustrated; problems which include lack of integrity in government; the feeling that the individual no longer counts; the reality of material and spiritual poverty; the feeling that the grand American experiment is failing or has failed. I could recite these problems and then I could sit down and offer no solutions. But I don't choose to do that either.

The citizens of America expect more. They deserve and they want more than a recital of problems.

We are a people in a quandary about the present. We are a people in search of our future. We are a people in search of a national community.

She then turned to her own Democratic Party and asked, "What is it about the Democratic Party that makes it the instrument that people use when they search for ways to shape their future?"

She answered that question this way:

We believe in equality for all and privileges for none.

We believe that the people are the source of all governmental power.

We are a party of innovation.

We have a positive vision of the future founded on the belief that the gap between the promise and reality of America can one day be finally closed.

Let's all understand that these guiding principles cannot be discarded for short-term political gains. They represent what this country is all about. They are indigenous to the American [ideal]. And these are principles which are not negotiable.

Because Barbara Jordan was the first African American woman to make a keynote address to the national convention of a major political party, her challenge toward the end of this 1976 speech should apply equally to Democrats and to Republicans in 2007:

If we promise . . . we must deliver.

If we propose . . . we must produce.

If we say to the American people it is time for you to be sacrificial, [we must] sacrifice.

. . . If we make mistakes, we must be willing to admit them.

Barbara Jordan was preaching to Democrats in 1976, and through her words in text and on DVD she is once again preaching to a nation.

Delivering the keynote address to the Democratic National Convention, July 12, 1976. Photograph by Warren K. Leffler, *U.S. News and World Report*, July 11–12, 1976. *U.S. News and World Report* Collection, Prints and Photographs Division. LC-U9-32937, frame 32A-33.

DEMOCRATIC NATIONAL CONVENTION KEYNOTE ADDRESS, NEW YORK, JULY 12, 1976

WHO THEN WILL SPEAK FOR THE COMMON GOOD?

Thank you, ladies and gentlemen, for a very warm reception.

It was one hundred and forty-four years ago that members of the Democratic Party first met in convention to select a presidential candidate. Since that time, Democrats have continued to convene once every four years and draft a party platform and nominate a presidential candidate. And our meeting this week is a continuation of that tradition.

But there is something different about tonight. There is something special about tonight. What is different? What is special? I, Barbara Jordan, am a keynote speaker.

A lot of years have passed since 1832, and during that time it would have been most unusual for any national political party to ask a Barbara Jordan to deliver a keynote address. But tonight, here I am. And I feel that notwithstanding the past that my presence here is one additional bit of evidence that the American Dream need not forever be deferred.

Now that I have this grand distinction, what in the world am I supposed to say?

I could easily spend this time praising the accomplishments of this party and attacking the Republicans.

But I don't choose to do that.

I could list the many problems which Americans have. I could list the problems which cause people to feel cynical, angry, frustrated: problems which include lack of integrity in government;

the feeling that the individual no longer counts; the reality of material and spiritual poverty; the feeling that the grand American experiment is failing or has failed. I could recite these problems, and then I could sit down and offer no solutions. But I don't choose to do that either.

The citizens of America expect more. They deserve and they want more than a recital of problems.

We are a people in a quandary about the present. We are a people in search of our future. We are a people in search of a national community.

We are a people trying not only to solve the problems of the present: unemployment, inflation—but we are attempting on a larger scale to fulfill the promise of America. We are attempting to fulfill our national purpose, to create and sustain a society in which all of us are equal.

Throughout our history, when people have looked for new ways to solve their problems, and to uphold the principles of this nation, many times they have turned to political parties. They have often turned to the Democratic Party.

What is it, what is it about the Democratic Party that makes it the instrument the people use when they search for ways to shape their future? Well, I believe the answer to that question lies in our concept of governing. Our concept of governing is derived from our view of people. It is a concept deeply rooted in a set of beliefs firmly etched in the national conscience of all of us.

Now what are these beliefs?

First, we believe in equality for all and privileges for none. This is a belief that each American, regardless of background, has equal standing in the public forum, all of us. Because we believe this idea so firmly, we are an inclusive rather than an exclusive party. Let everybody come.

I think it no accident that most of those immigrating to America in the nineteenth century identified with the Democratic Party. We are a heterogeneous party made up of Americans of diverse backgrounds.

We believe that the people are the source of all governmental power; that the authority of the people is to be extended, not restricted. This can be accomplished only by providing each citizen with every opportunity to participate in the management of the government. They must have that.

We believe that the government which represents the authority of all the people, not just one interest group, but all the people, has an obligation to actively underscore, actively seek to remove those obstacles which would block, *individual achievement,* obstacles emanating from race, sex, economic condition. The government must remove them. Seek to remove them.

We are a party of innovation. We do not reject our traditions, but we are willing to adapt to changing circumstances, when change we must. We are willing to suffer the discomfort of change in order to achieve a better future.

We have a positive vision of the future founded on the belief that the gap between the promise and reality of America can one day be finally closed. We believe that.

This, my friends, is the bedrock of our concept of governing. This is a part of the reason why Americans have turned to the Democratic Party. These are the foundations upon which a national community can be built.

Let all understand that these guiding principles cannot be discarded for short-term political gains. They represent what this country is all about. They are indigenous to the American idea. And these are principles which are not negotiable.

In other times, I could stand here and give this kind of exposition on the beliefs of the Democratic Party and that would be enough. But today that is not enough. People want more. That is not sufficient reason for the majority of the people of this country to decide to vote Democratic. We have made mistakes. We have made mistakes. We realize that. We admit our mistakes. In our haste to do all things for all people, we did not foresee the full consequences of our actions. And when the people raised their voices, we didn't hear. But our deafness was only a temporary condition, and not an irreversible condition.

Even as I stand here and admit that we have made mistakes, I still believe that as the people of America sit in judgment on each party, they will recognize that our mistakes were mistakes of the heart. They'll recognize that.

And now we must look to the future. Let us heed the voice of the people and recognize their common sense. If we do not, we not only blaspheme our political heritage, we ignore the common ties that bind all Americans.

Many fear the future. Many are distrustful of their leaders, and believe that their voices are never heard. Many seek only to satisfy their private work wants. To satisfy their private interest.

But this is the great danger America faces. That we will cease to be one nation and become instead a collection of interest groups: city against suburb, region against region, individual against individual. Each seeking to satisfy private wants.

If that happens, who then will speak for America? Who then will speak for the common good? This is the question which must be answered in 1976.

Are we to be one people bound together by common spirit sharing in a common endeavor, or will we become a divided nation?

For all of its uncertainty, we cannot flee the future. We must not become the new Puritans and reject our society. We must address and master the future together. It can be done if we restore the belief that we share a sense of national community, that we share a common national endeavor. It can be done.

There is no executive order, there is no law, that can require the American people to form a national community. This we must do as individuals and if we do it as individuals, there is no president of the United States who can veto that decision.

As a first step, we must restore our belief in ourselves. We are a generous people, so why can't we be generous with each other? We need to take to heart the words spoken by Thomas Jefferson:

*Let us restore to social intercourse that harmony and that affec-
tion without which liberty and even life are but dreary things.*

A nation is formed by the willingness of each of us to share in
the responsibility for upholding the common good.

A government is invigorated when each one of us is willing to
participate in shaping the future of this nation.

In this election year, we must define the common good and
begin again to shape a common future. Let each person do his
or her part. If one citizen is unwilling to participate, all of us are
going to suffer. For the American ideal, though it is shared by all
of us, is realized in each one of us.

And now, what are those of us who are elected public officials
supposed to do? We call ourselves public servants, but I'll tell you
this: we as public servants must set an example for the rest of the
nation. It is hypocritical for the public official to admonish and
exhort the people to uphold the common good if we are derelict
in upholding the common good. More is required of public officials than slogans and handshakes and press releases. More is
required. We must hold ourselves strictly accountable. We must
provide the people with a vision of the future.

If we promise as public officials, we must deliver. If we, as public officials, propose, we must produce. If we say to the American
people, "it is time for you to be sacrificial," sacrifice. If the public
official says that, we must be the first to give. We must be. And
again, if we make mistakes, we must be willing to admit them.
We have to do that. What we have to do is strike a balance between the idea that government should do everything, and the
idea, the belief, that government ought to do nothing. Strike a
balance.

Let there be no illusions about the difficulty of forming this
kind of a national community. It's tough, difficult, not easy. But
a spirit of harmony will survive in America only if each of us
remembers that we share a common destiny.

If each of us remembers when self-interest and bitterness seem to prevail, that we share a common destiny, I have confidence that we can form this kind of national community.

I have confidence that the Democratic Party can lead the way. I have that confidence. We cannot improve on the system of government handed down to us by the founders of the republic; there is no way to improve upon that. But what we can do is to find new ways to implement that system and realize our destiny.

Now, I began this speech by commenting to you on the uniqueness of a Barbara Jordan making a keynote address. Well, I am going to close my speech by quoting a Republican president, and I ask you that as you listen to these words of Abraham Lincoln, relate them to the concept of national community in which every last one of us participates: "As I would not be a slave, so I would not be a master."

This expresses my idea of democracy. Whatever differs from this, to the extent of the difference, is no democracy.

THE SPOTLIGHT AFTER CONGRESS

IN 1992, SIXTEEN YEARS AFTER HER HISTORIC 1976 KEYNOTE address, Professor Barbara Jordan returned to New York City to keynote another Democratic National Convention. The tone of this speech was more somber, but her prophetic words again seemed to be prepared for the year 2008. Here are just three exemplary excerpts:

> *Friends of the Democratic Party, the American Dream is not dead. It is not dead! It is gasping for breath, but it is not dead. We can applaud that statement and know that there is no time to waste because the American Dream is slipping away from too many people. It is slipping away from too many black and brown mothers and their children. The American Dream is slipping away from the homeless—of every color and of every sex. It's slipping away from those immigrants living in communities without water and sewage systems. The American Dream is slipping away from those persons who have jobs, jobs which no longer will pay the benefits which will enable them to live and thrive because America seems to be better at building war equipment to sit in warehouses and rot than in building decent housing. It's slipping away. It's slipping away.*

> *"E Pluribus Unum"—"from many, one." It was a good idea when [the country] was founded, and it's a good idea today.*

> *We must change that deleterious environment of the eighties, that environment which was characterized by greed, and hatred, and selfishness, and mega-mergers, and debt overhang. Change it to what? Change that environment of the eighties to an environment which is characterized by a devotion to the public interest, public service, tolerance, and love. Love. Love. Love.*

Barbara Jordan deeply believed that "liberty lies in the hearts of men and women." She did not hesitate to speak to the heart. When she emphasized and reemphasized love, she reaffirmed her belief "that there may be a kingdom where the least shall be heard and considered side by side with the greatest."

This was Barbara Jordan's last speech before a national television audience.

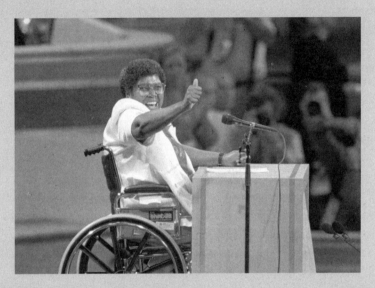

Barbara Jordan at the Democratic National Convention, July 13, 1992. Photo courtesy of the *Houston Chronicle*.

CHANGE: FROM WHAT TO WHAT?

It was at this time. It was at this place. It was at this event six-teen years ago, I presented a keynote address to the Democratic National Convention. I remind you, with modesty, I remind you that that year, 1976, we won the presidency. Why not repeat that performance in 1992? We can do it. We can do it. We can do it.

What we need to do, Democrats, is believe that it is possible to win. It is possible. We can do it. Now, you have heard a lot about change tonight. Every speaker here has said something about change. And I want you to talk with me for a few minutes about change. But I want you to listen to the way I have entitled my remarks—"Change: From What to What?" From what to what? This change—which is very rhetorically oriented—this change acquires substance when each of us contemplates the public mind. What about the public mind?

There appears to be a general apprehension in the country about the future. That apprehension undermines our faith in each other and our faith in ourselves. Undermines that confidence. The idea that America today will be better tomorrow has become destabilized. It has become destabilized because of the recession and the sluggishness of the economy. Jobs lost have become per-manent unemployment rather than cyclical unemployment. The public mind. Public policy makers are held in low regard. Mis-trust abounds. In this kind of environment, it is understandable that *change* would become the watchword of this time.

What is the catalyst which will bring about the change we're all talking about? I say that catalyst is the Democratic Party and our nominee for president.

We are not strangers to change. Twenty years ago, we changed the whole tone of the nation after Watergate abuses. We did that twenty years ago. We know how to change. We have been the instrument of change in the past. We know what needs to be done. We know how to do it. We know that we can impact policies which affect education, human rights, civil rights, economic and social opportunity, and the environment.

These are policies, these are policies, which are imbedded in the soul of the Democratic Party, and imbedded in our soul they will not disappear easily. We as a party will do nothing to erode our essence. We will not.

But there are some things which ought to change, we need to change them, but the fact that we are going to change things should not cause any apprehension in our minds, because the Democratic Party is alive and well. It is alive and well. We will change in order to satisfy the present, in order to satisfy the future, but we will not die. We will change, but we will not die.

From what to what? Why not change from a party with a reputation of "tax and spend" to one with a reputation of "investment and growth"? Change. Change. A growth economy is a must. We can grow the economy and sustain an improved environment at the same time. When the economy is growing and we are taking care of our air and soil and water, we all prosper. And we can do all of that.

When I say something like that, I certainly do not mean the thinly disguised racism and elitism which is some kind of trickle-down economics. I'll tell you, I will tell you the kind of economy I'm talking about. I'm talking about an economy where a young black woman or a young black man, born in the Fifth Ward of Houston—my town—or South Central Los Angeles, or a young person in the *colonias* of the lower Rio Grande valley—I'm talking about an economy where those persons can go to a public school, learn the skills that will enable her or him to prosper.

We must have an economy that does not force that migrant worker's child to miss school for a full day so that she can work at less than the minimum wage—and doing that, the family can still only afford one meal a day. That is the moral bankruptcy of trickle-down economics. Change. Change. Change.

We can change the direction of America's economic engine and become competitive again. We can make that change and become proud of the country that we are.

Friends in the Democratic Party, the American Dream is not dead. It is not dead! It is gasping for breath, but it is not dead. We can applaud that statement and know that there is no time to waste because the American Dream is slipping away from too many people. It is slipping away from too many black and brown mothers and their children. The American Dream is slipping away from the homeless—of every color, of every sex. It's slipping away from those immigrants living in communities without water and sewage systems. The American Dream is slipping away from those persons who have jobs, jobs which no longer will pay the benefits which will enable them to live and thrive because America seems to be better at building war equipment to sit in warehouses and rot than in building decent housing. It's slipping away. It's slipping away.

The American Dream is slipping away from those workers who are on indefinite layoffs while their chief executive officers are taking home bonuses which equal more than the worker will ever make in ten, twenty, or thirty years.

We need to change the decaying inner cities from decay—to places where hope lives. As we undergo that change, we must be prepared to answer Rodney King's haunting question, "Can we all get along?" "Can we all get along?" I say—I say, we answer that question with a resounding "Yes!" Yes. Yes.

We must change that deleterious environment of the eighties, that environment which was characterized by greed, and hatred, and selfishness, and mega-mergers, and debt overhangs. Change it to what? Change that environment of the eighties to an environment which is characterized by a devotion to the public interest, public service, tolerance, and love. Love. Love. Love.

We are one, we Americans. We're one and we reject any intruder who seeks to divide us on the basis of race and color. We honor cultural identity. We always have; we always will. But separatism is not allowed. Separatism is not the American way. We must not allow ideas like political correctness to divide us and cause us to reverse hard-won achievements in human rights and civil rights. Xenophobia has no place in the Democratic Party.

We seek to unite people, not divide them. As we seek to unite people, we reject both white racism and black racism. This party will not tolerate bigotry under any guise.

Our strength in this country is rooted in our diversity. Our history bears witness to that fact. "E Pluribus Unum"—"from many, one." It was a good idea when it was founded, and it's a good idea today. From many, one. That still identifies us. We must frankly acknowledge our complicity in the creation of the unconscionable budget deficits—acknowledge our complicity and recognize, painful though it may be, that in order to seriously address the budget deficits, we must address the question of entitlements also. That's not easy. That's not easy. But we have to do it; we have to do it; because the idea of justice between generations, that idea mandates that the baby-boomers—that's our ticket—the baby-boomers and their progeny are entitled to a secure future. They are.

However, if we are going to ask those who receive benefits to sacrifice, there must be equity in sacrifice. Equity in sacrifice. That idea says that we will sacrifice for growth, but that everybody must join in the sacrifice, not just a few. Equity in sacrifice means that all will sacrifice equally . . . equally . . . equally. That is, the person who is retired on a fixed income, the day laborer, the corporate executive, the college professor, the member of congress—all must sacrifice for equity.

One overdue change, which you have already heard a lot about, is already underway. And that is reflected in the number of women now challenging the councils of political power. These women are challenging those councils of political power because they have been dominated by white, male policymakers, and that is wrong. That horizon of gender equity is limitless for us. And what we see today is simply a dress rehearsal for the day and time we meet in convention to nominate Madame President. This country can ill afford to continue to function using less than half its human resources, less than half its kinetic energy, less than half its brain power.

We had a nineteenth-century visitor from France named de Tocqueville. De Tocqueville came to America, and he was asked—"If I were asked"—this is de Tocqueville—"If I were asked," he said, "to what singular substance do I mainly attribute the prosperity and growing strength of the American people, I should reply," de Tocqueville said, "I should reply: To the superiority of their women." I can only say the twentieth century will not close without the presence of women being keenly felt.

We must leave this convention tonight with a determination to convince the American people to trust us. The American electorate must be persuaded to trust us, the Democrats, to govern again. That is not easy, but we can do it. We can do it.

Public apprehension and fears about the future have provided very fertile ground for a chorus of cynics. And these cynics go around saying that it makes no difference who is elected president of the United States. You must say to those cynics, "You are perpetuating a fraud." It *does* make a difference who is president. A Democratic president would appoint a Supreme Court justice who protects liberty, rather than burden liberty. A Democratic president would promote principles, programs, policies which help us help ourselves.

Now, there is another agenda item which has arisen. *Character* has become an item on the political agenda of 1992. The question of character is a proper one, but if you were to exercise a well-reasoned examination, a well-reasoned examination of the question of character, what you discover is that the whole question falls into emotionalism rather than fact. You know how dangerous it is to make decisions based on emotion, rather than reason. James Madison, the founder of the Constitution, the father of the Constitution, warned us of the perils of relying on passion rather than reason.

There is an editor, a late editor of the Emporia, Kansas, *Gazette*—William White—who had this to say about reason, and it's very, very pertinent. The quote: "Reason has never failed man. Only fear and oppression have made the wrecks of the world." It is reason; it is reason; it is reason and not passion which should guide our decisions.

The question persists: Who can best lead this country at this moment in our history?

I close my remarks by quoting from Franklin Roosevelt— Franklin Roosevelt's inaugural address, which he made in 1933. Franklin Roosevelt made that address to a people longing for change from the darkness and despair of the Great Depression. And this is what Roosevelt said:

> *In every dark hour of our national life a leadership of frankness and vigor has met with that understanding and support of the people themselves which is essential to victory.*

Given the ingredients of today's national environment, maybe, maybe, just maybe, we Americans are poised for a second "Rendezvous with Destiny."

BARBARA JORDAN'S TAKE ON THREE TWENTY-FIRST-CENTURY POLITICAL ISSUES

CONFIRMATION OF
SUPREME COURT JUSTICES

BARBARA JORDAN'S "TESTIMONY IN OPPOSITION TO THE Nomination of Robert Bork," delivered to the United States Senate Committee on the Judiciary on September 17, 1987, is a roadmap of a reasoned and responsible basis for opposing a presidential nominee to the United States Supreme Court. At the outset of her brief remarks, she assured the committee that her opposition was "not a knee-jerk reaction of 'follower-ship' of persons and groups whose views I generally share." Rather, her strong opposition was based on careful thought and personal experience.

Barbara's personal story is that of a young African American lawyer who in 1963 returned home from law school in Boston to run for a seat in the Texas House of Representatives, seeking one of the at-large seats to be filled from Houston, in Harris County. In 1962 she received 46,000 votes but was not elected; in 1964 she received 64,000 votes but again lost. She asked, "Why couldn't I win? Those were countywide races in which the votes of the people who knew me were diluted by the votes of people who didn't know me. I was dispirited. I was trying to play by the rules, but the rules were not fair."

The rules began to change when legislative reapportionment was forced on the states by the U.S. Supreme Court in such landmark cases as *Baker v. Carr* in 1962, which held that the question of legislative reapportionment was a proper issue to be decided by the courts, and *Reynolds v. Sims* in 1964, which held that districts in both houses of a bicameral legislature must be as nearly of equal population as practicable. In 1965 a three-judge federal court in *Kilgarlin v. Martin* ordered the Texas Legislature to redraw house and senate districts to conform to the new "one person, one vote" rule. The court also struck down two provisions of the Texas Constitution—one that limited a county to one state senator and another that prevented any county from having more than seven members in the Texas House of Representatives. The Texas Legislature did reapportion, and in 1966 Barbara Jordan ran successfully for a seat in the State Senate.[6]

Barbara testified that Robert Bork had said that *Baker v. Carr* was wrongly decided, as was the Supreme Court case that outlawed the poll tax. There is much more to her testimony, but the consequence of "Bork-ian" reasoning was clear to her: "My eyes glaze over when I think about what would be if there were no *Baker v. Carr*. I would now be running my eleventh unsuccessful race for the State House."

Barbara Jordan's testimony is a sterling example of opposition to a Supreme Court nominee based on his record and sound reasons. The corresponding footage on the enclosed DVD is a must-see, from start to finish.

Speaking at the LBJ Library, May 7, 1986. LBJ Library photo by Frank Wolf, courtesy of the Lyndon B. Johnson Presidential Library, Austin.

TESTIMONY IN OPPOSITION TO THE NOMINATION OF ROBERT BORK, STATEMENT TO THE COMMITTEE ON THE JUDICIARY, SEPTEMBER 17, 1987

Mr. Chairman:

I oppose the nomination of Robert Bork to the Supreme Court of the United States. My opposition is not a knee-jerk reaction of follower-ship of persons and groups whose views I generally share. My opposition is the result of careful thought, a reading of the White House position paper in support of Judge Bork and this committee's point-by-point response, discussions with persons whose views I respect, and fifty-one years of being a Black American, born in the South and determined to be heard by the majority community. Those factors caused me to become an opponent.

Mr. Chairman, I concede the nominee's quality of intellect and scholarship. But more is required. When you have experienced the frustrations of the minority position and felt the foreclosure of your last appeal, to be rescued by a decision of the Supreme Court of the United States is like being born again. I had that experience. The year was 1962. I had recently graduated from Boston University Law School (1959). A group of local Democrats urged me to run for election to the Texas House of Representatives. There were twelve places to be filled from Houston, Harris County, Texas. I sought Place 10. I lost, but I got 46,000 votes. Undaunted, I ran again in 1964, thinking people know me now. Again I lost, but I got over 64,000 votes. Why couldn't I win? Those were countywide races in which the votes of the people who knew me were diluted by the votes of people who didn't know me. I was *dispirited*. I was trying to play by the rules, but the rules were not fair. Enter now the Supreme Court decision called *Baker v. Carr*. The court held that "the complainants' allegations of a denial of equal protection present a justiciable constitutional cause of action. The right asserted is within the reach of judicial protection under the Fourteenth Amendment."

There followed a series of cases with respect to having votes count equally. The Texas Legislature was required to reapportion itself. In 1966 I ran for the Texas State Senate in one of the newly created districts, and this time I won. Judge Bork has repeatedly voiced his disagreement with the decisions establishing the principle of one person, one vote. In his confirmation hearings in 1973, he said, "I think one man, one vote was too much of a straight jacket. I do not think there is a theoretical basis for it." Well, maybe not. Maybe not. But there is a natural and common-sense basis for it.

We once had a poll tax in Texas. It was used to keep people from voting. The Supreme Court said it was wrong and outlawed it. Robert Bork said the case was wrongly decided.

The right to privacy has been recognized and confirmed in landmark Supreme Court cases from *Griswold* to *Roe v. Wade* and beyond. Robert Bork recognizes no such constitutional right. It is his belief that if a right is not explicitly found in the letter of the Constitution then it does not exist. And further, for the courts to find and define such a right is a usurpation of the role of democratically elected state legislative bodies. In my opinion that is a dangerous view to have on the Supreme Court. I want to continue to see the court as the last bulwark of protection of our freedoms.

The presence of Robert Bork on the court places that in jeopardy. Further, that position regarding rights is on its face inconsistent with the whole of the Constitution. The Ninth Amendment to the Constitution states, "The enumeration in the Constitution of certain rights shall not be construed to deny or disparage others retained by the people." The people are the source of certain rights and that is an undeniable Constitutional fact. The Declaration of Independence preceded the Constitution. That document states that we are endowed by our Creator with certain inalienable rights. Among these are life, liberty, and the pursuit of happiness. I state "among these" for emphasis, the inference being, there are others. A Borkian or originalist would counter with: These rights are to be secured by elected, legislative bodies. My eyes glaze over when I think about what would be if there were no *Baker v. Carr.* I would now be running my eleventh unsuccessful race for the State House.

The White House position paper tells us everything we ever needed to know about Bork's role in the Saturday Night Massacre except that the action of Robert Bork in firing Archibald Cox, special prosecutor, was illegal. It was so held in the decision which arose out of this matter.

With the office of special prosecutor/independent counsel being under attack by the Justice Department and others, this is the wrong time and sends the wrong signal to confirm to the Supreme Court one who has shown such utter disdain for the office.

Our belief in the Constitution is a part of our cultural glue. The Supreme Court should be a ballast helping to keep the Ship of State from making wide, unanticipated swings. The new justice will be the determinant of whether we stay the course or turn abruptly away from societal gains hard won.

Therefore, Robert Bork should not be confirmed.

IMMIGRATION REFORM

WHEN PRESIDENT CLINTON APPOINTED BARBARA JORDAN TO chair the U.S. Commission on Immigration Reform (CIR) on December 14, 1993, he gave this reason for choosing her:

> I have chosen Barbara Jordan—one of the most well-respected people in America—to chair this commission because immigration is one of the most important and complex issues facing our country today.[7]

Barbara Jordan chaired the commission through 1994 and several months of 1995. She died before the final report of September 30, 1997. She accepted the appointment "because she believed that debate about immigration policy and reform of its problem areas were necessary if we were to retain our strong tradition as a nation of immigrants committed to the rule of law."[8]

Prior to her death, Barbara testified about the work of the CIR before congressional committees. This, her last major undertaking, was a controversial report because it drew a sharp distinction between legal and illegal immigration. Hispanic leaders disagreed with her over commission recommendations, but as one prominent Hispanic leader said at the time of her death: "This doesn't take away from her greatness in our community. She left her mark on this country." Barbara Jordan shows us that a leader can take principled, controversial positions, and still be respected and followed.

The work of the CIR is a case study of civility in government. When testifying before one of the congressional committees, she had these words:

> We are a bipartisan group composed of nine members. I was ap-

pointed ... by President Clinton. My eight colleagues were ap-
pointed by the Democratic and Republican leadership of the two
houses of Congress.

Our work has not been easy. Distinguishing fact from fiction
has been almost impossible, because of what has become a high-
ly emotional debate on immigration. We have heard contradictory
testimony, shaky statistics, and a great deal of honest confusion
regarding the impacts of immigration. Nevertheless, we have tried
throughout to engage in what we believe is a systematic, nonpar-
tisan effort to reach conclusions drawn from analysis of the best
data available. The recommendations that I present today have
been adopted unanimously.[9]

This nonpartisan effort is the way government is supposed to work,
once the elections are over. Barbara Jordan's leadership on this highly
charged issue is reminiscent of what Lyndon Johnson, as Senate Majority
Leader, and Sam Rayburn, as Speaker of the House—both Democrats—
did immediately after the election of the very popular Dwight Eisenhower
in 1952. They offered to help him as often as they could and to oppose
him only when he tried to undo "the good things we Democrats did" in
the New and Fair Deals. "[T]he adage that the opposition's duty was to
oppose was not Rayburn's adage. He didn't want to oppose simply for
the sake of opposing. 'Any jackass can kick a barn down,' he said. 'But it
takes a good carpenter to build one.'"[10]

On March 29, 1995, less than a year before her death, Barbara Jordan
testified before a subcommittee of the U.S. House of Representatives
Committee on Appropriations. Fortunately, that testimony was recorded
so that summary recommendations on the difficult issue of immigration
reform are available in text.

With President Bill Clinton during the ceremony in which Jordan received the
Presidential Medal of Freedom, 1994. Photo courtesy of Barbara Jordan Archives,
Robert James Terry Library, Texas Southern University, Houston.

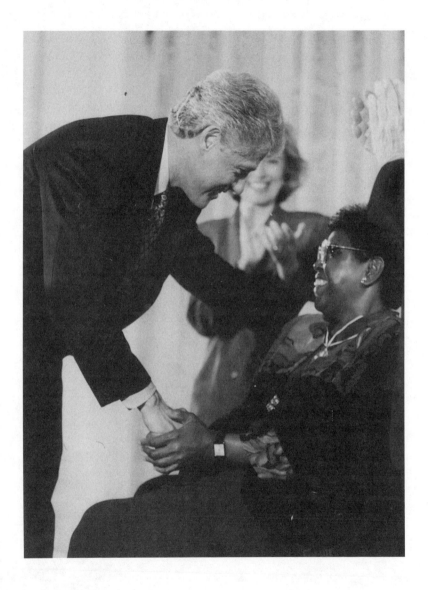

CONGRESSIONAL TESTIMONY AS CHAIR OF THE U.S. COMMISSION ON IMMIGRATION REFORM, MARCH 29, 1995

Mr. Chairman, members of the subcommittee, thank you for providing this opportunity to testify today. I am Barbara Jordan, the chair of the Commission on Immigration Reform. I am accompanied by the commission's executive director, Susan Martin.

Before I begin my formal testimony, I must commend this committee on its use of new technology to bring the work of the Congress closer to the American people. As you will hear later in my testimony, the commission shares your belief that the federal government must tap new technologies in order to make the work of government efficient and in touch with the demands of the American public.

The Commission on Immigration Reform was created by the Immigration Act of 1990. We are a fully bipartisan body. In addition to the chair, we have eight members who were appointed by the majority and minority leadership in each house of Congress.

The commission's mandate is to examine and make recommendations to this Congress on the implementation and impact of U.S. immigration policy. We are required to make interim reports as issues arise and a final report in September 1997. The Commission issued its first interim report in September 1994. In calendar year 1995, we intend to issue three reports with interim recommendations on a range of issues from legal immigration numbers and categories to the handling of migration emergencies and the removal of deportable aliens from the United States. In addition, we continue to pursue our long-term agenda to assess the economic, social, demographic, and other impacts of immigration on the United States.

This morning I would like to describe briefly the recommendations the commission already has made in the hopes that they will be useful to this committee in setting FY 1995 appropriations not only for the commission, but also for other immigration-related agencies. I will then turn to our plans for this fiscal year and our request for next year's appropriations.

The commission's 1994 report to Congress was entitled *U.S. Immigration Policy: Restoring Credibility.* The title is telling of our recommendations. The commission believes it is essential to control illegal immigration if we are to have a credible immigration policy. We believe legal immigration is in the national interest, but see illegal immigration as a threat both to our long tradition of immigration and to our commitment to the rule of law.

The commission recommends a comprehensive, seven-point strategy to restore credibility. Let me tell you that the strategy is neither cheap nor painless. There are no quick fixes to our immigration problems; there are no inexpensive solutions. For too long we have neglected immigration as a public policy issue and now must pay for the consequences.

Four points in our report call for special attention. First, we need improved border management. The commission calls for a strategy of prevention of illegal entry and facilitation of legal ones in the national interest. The concept is simpler, of course, than its achievement. The commission was highly impressed with the border operations in El Paso that aim to prevent illegal entry. It is far better to deter illegal immigration than to play the cat-and-mouse game that results from apprehensions followed by return followed by reentry. To accomplish a true deterrence strategy will require additional personnel as well as a strategic use of technology and equipment. We will also require new measures of effectiveness because apprehensions alone cannot measure success in preventing illegal entries. Our goal should be zero apprehensions—not because aliens get past the Border Patrol but because they are prevented entry in the first place.

While we tighten our control over illegal entry, we must also reduce the long waiting times at our ports of entry. It is ridiculous that people with legitimate border crossing cards feel it is more convenient to cross illegally than go through our ports of entry. But that is the case. Our own delegation waited for one and one-half hours to cross from Juárez into El Paso—and this wasn't even at rush hour. In an age of NAFTA, we must do a better job of handling the legitimate border travel. The commission supports the development of a land border user fee whose resources would be used to open more lanes, add more inspectors, and, if necessary, more ports of entry to speed this traffic.

Our second set of recommendations would reduce the magnet that jobs currently present for illegal immigration. We have concluded that illegal immigrants come primarily for employment. The commission believes that we need to enhance our enforcement of both employer sanctions and labor standards. But, to make employer sanctions work, we must improve the means by which employers verify the work authorization of new employees. The commission believes the most promising option is a computerized system for determining if a social security number is valid and has been issued to someone authorized to work in the United States. We are pleased that the administration has endorsed our recommendations in this area, and we look forward to working with INS and the Social Security Administration on the design of pilot programs that will phase in and test this new verification approach. I urge this committee to provide the funding needed to develop the computerized system and implement the pilot programs.

Third, the commission urges greater consistency in our immigration and benefits policies. We believe that illegal aliens should be eligible for no public benefits other than those of an emergency nature, in the public health and safety interest, and constitutionally protected. On the other hand, we urge the Congress to retain for legal immigrants eligibility for our safety net programs. The United States screens legal immigrants to determine if they will become public charges, but unforeseen circumstances—deaths, illnesses—occur. The commission does not want to see individuals whom we have invited to enter become vulnerable when such situations arise. On the other hand, the commission strongly supports efforts to make our public charge provisions work. We do not want the U.S. taxpayer to bear a burden when there is a sponsor in this country who has pledged to provide support for an immigrant. The affidavits of support signed by sponsors should be legally binding, and the provisions for deportation of those who do become a public charge—for reasons known prior to entry—should be strengthened.

The commission also made recommendations regarding impact aid for states and localities experiencing the fiscal effects of illegal immigration. We believe the federal government has a responsibility in this area. The first responsibility is to control illegal entries; the second is to help states and localities with their fiscal problems. However, we are skeptical of some of the data used to calculate these fiscal impacts. At present, the commission believes that the data to support reimbursement of criminal justice costs are sound, and we urge immediate reimbursement of these costs. We are not prepared to make such a recommendation regarding medical and education costs. We also urge that any impact aid provided require appropriate cooperation by states and localities in the enforcement of immigration policy.

Our fourth area concerns the removal of criminal aliens. The commission supports enhancement of the Institutional Hearing Program that permits the federal government to obtain a deportation order while criminal aliens are still serving their sentences. Once the sentence is over, it is far easier and less expensive to remove the alien after an IHP proceeding. The commission also recommends further negotiation of bilateral treaties that will permit deportation of criminal aliens to serve their sentences in their home countries.

The commission has provided copies of our full report to the committee so I will not go into details on the other recommendations. Let me turn my attention to this year's work. The commission is currently at work on three reports while engaging in research needed to answer the longer-term questions in our legislative mandate. Our budget justification spells out these reports in some detail, so let me emphasize our work in only one of these areas: legal immigration.

At the request of the House and Senate Judiciary Committees, the commission has accelerated its examination of the legal immigration system in order to make recommendations by June 1. Last week, we spent a day of executive session debating basic principles to underlie our legal immigration policies. We discussed the national interest in family reunification; employment-based immigration; and diversity, refugee, and humanitarian admissions and we set out the objectives that each of us wants from legal immigration. During the next two months, we turn our attention to the numbers and criteria for admission that fulfill these objectives, the procedures we use to determine the admissibility of individuals applying for permanent and temporary admission, and other similar issues.

We are also looking at naturalization and the civic integration of newcomers to the United States. I, for one, would like to see all eligible immigrants become U.S. citizens—and become citizens for the right reasons, not to receive some federal benefit but to be fully participating members of our polity. Right now, there are too many barriers to naturalization. In some districts, it can take two years to complete the process. We plan to have recommendations to improve this situation.

Now, for FY 1996. We have requested an increase in appropriations for next fiscal year because we see a significant increase in our work. We expect and support major administrative and legislative action this year on immigration reform. The commission feels an obligation to monitor the implementation of these initiatives so that we can give an independent assessment to the Congress of their effectiveness in reducing illegal immigration.

In addition to these assessments, the commission will also turn its attention to structural issues in the implementation of U.S. immigration policy. Having made interim recommendations on improvements we urge regarding both legal and illegal immigration, the commission will examine the adequacy of the structures we have in place to implement such policy. In our 1994 report, we already raised a number of questions regarding implementation and coordination of policy. For example, we have concerns about our border management apparatus, the coordination between the INS and the Department of Labor in worksite investigations, and the infrastructure to support effective enforcement and service delivery. These and other similar issues will be the focus of our attention in the next fiscal year. The commission also will continue its assessment of the labor market, fiscal, social, and demographic impacts of immigration, as required by our statutory mandate. We already have begun two major, two-year research initiatives that will provide cutting-edge information on these issues. One is an expert panel at the National Academy of Sciences to assess the literature on the demographic, labor market, and fiscal effects of immigration, to undertake new research to fill gaps in current understanding, and to report to the commission on their conclusions regarding the short-term and long-term implications of immigration for U.S. society. The second is a binational study with Mexico that should provide new information on the scale, characteristics, and impact of the largest single source of both legal and illegal immigration to this country. This binational study will permit data collection in both countries, providing answers to questions that cannot be examined adequately with data from the United States alone.

I thank you again for this opportunity to discuss the work and recommendations of the Commission on Immigration Reform.

I also want to state for the record our commitment to work with this committee as you address the very challenging issues arising in the appropriation of funds to improve implementation of immigration policy. We are the creation of Congress and offer ourselves as a resource to help you in your work. Dr. Martin and I would be pleased to answer questions.

RELIGIOUS FAITH AND POLITICS

AS A "CHILD OF THE MANSE," FAITH WAS IMPORTANT TO
Barbara Jordan. In 1978 Congresswoman Jordan gave the opening prayer
for the National Prayer Breakfast in Washington, D.C. In 1984 Professor
Jordan was the main speaker for the National Prayer Breakfast, along
with newly elected President Ronald Reagan. Here are a few of her words:
"Know that here on earth God's work must truly be our own."

She pointed out to that huge audience that those were the closing
words of President John F. Kennedy's inaugural address. She then asked
the attendees, political leaders, these questions:

> Would we behave as we do . . . if we truly believed that we are
> God's stewards on this earth? Would our policy decisions be the
> same . . . if we were always consciously aware of our trusteeship
> role on this earth? Would our oversight responsibilities be sharper,
> more incisive, if we believed that we are God's caretakers?

She then focused on two core values for people of faith that to her
are nonnegotiable. Justice, which she called the "flagship principle" and
"the highest ideal for society," was to her very simple. It is where "everyone is treated fairly by everyone else." Selflessness, which she acknowl-
edged is difficult to attain, especially in a landscape of acquisitiveness,
profits, competition, and progress, is the other core value.

She concludes this way: "Let us go forth and lead the land we love,
asking [God's] blessing and [God's] help, but knowing that here on earth
God's work must truly be our own."

I regret that neither an audio nor video recording of her remarks at
the National Prayer Breakfast is available. The text of her 1978 prayer
and her 1984 speech, recorded in the February 22, 1984, *Congressional
Record—Senate,* do give an insight into how Barbara Jordan balanced
political leadership with religious faith.

With President Jimmy Carter. Photo courtesy of Barbara Jordan Archives,
Robert James Terry Library, Texas Southern University, Houston.

PRAYER AT THE NATIONAL PRAYER BREAKFAST, WASHINGTON, D.C., FEBRUARY 2, 1978

Let us bow our heads, close our eyes, and open our hearts to the one who is greater than we.

We are so human and inadequate to the task which is ours: to serve as your trustees for the benefit of your people. Help us to be mindful that we are not alone. When we need wisdom, we need only to ask for it. You have promised to bestow it liberally. When we are weak—and if we are patient—you will renew our strength. Strengthen us.

You know that we are ordinary and often find it difficult to love our neighbors as ourselves, but we know that if we fail to love, we fail not only our neighbors, but also you. When we succumb to hatred, greed, and self-centeredness, we give you cause to revoke the trust you have placed in us.

We beseech you to move so powerfully within us that we shall be able to avert sinfulness.

We do not serve as well as we might when we follow our own counsel rather than yours. Help us to trust in you rather than to rely totally on ourselves.

Teach us to know that if we are to be successful stewards, we must be your servants. We know that we cannot solve the many difficulties which beset your people. But *you* can. We cannot reconcile peoples whose prejudice and narrow-sighted self-interest prevent brotherhood. But *you* can. We cannot infuse hope in those who despair. But *you* can.

Since you can do all that we cannot do, give us the good sense to work with you in partnership for the benefit of all humankind. Help us to resist our inclination to be the senior partner. As we work together, keep talking to us and help us to listen.

Guide us in our decisions and grant us the wisdom, courage, and selflessness to discern the difference between good and bad, fact and fiction, reality and illusion.

ADDRESS AT THE NATIONAL PRAYER BREAKFAST, WASHINGTON, D.C., FEBRUARY 2, 1984

Thank you very much, Mr. President, Mrs. Reagan, Vice President Bush and Barbara Bush, and there are so many others. Members and officials and people of high office that I cannot acknowledge any further.

I am delighted to be here to deliver the message for this National Prayer Breakfast. I haven't given my remarks a subject, a title, but I will tell you what I am going to talk about. I am going to talk about the necessity for using, merging the inner life and the outer life, the inner self and the outer self.

When I told my colleagues at the University of Texas that that is what I was going to talk about, they said, "I hope there are no politicians where you're going."

And I said, "Why do you say that, sir?" He says, "Well, people who are in politics have been stripped of their inner lives. They don't have any, they are empty inside, they are slow, they are plastic."

I told him he was not telling the truth.

So let us begin. Knowing that here on earth God's work must truly be our own—knowing that here on earth God's work must truly be our own. Now, you will recognize those as the closing words of John Kennedy's inaugural address.

Would we behave as we do behave in word, thought, and deed if we truly believed that we are God's stewards on this earth? Would our policy decisions be the same that they are if we were always consciously aware of our trusteeship role on this earth?

Would our oversight responsibilities be sharper, more incisive if we believed that we are God's caretakers?

Our responses to these questions will reflect, will define how we relate our humanity to God. Your responses will also reflect the character and quality of your innate nature.

Shakespeare asks in one of his sonnets, what is your substance, whereof are you made. That's a big question. What is your substance? Whereof are you made? The answer to that question is not very simple.

Most of us would quickly retire to the Old Testament and say we are made in the image of God, and we would intone those words. But that response leaves too much unexplained. If we are made in the image of God, what is the source of our love of money? What is the source of our love of power? Profit? Wherein does greed and avarice and bitterness lie if you are made in the image of God? How do you explain your despoliation of the earth and propensity to rule over other men? How do we explain, if indeed we are made in the image of God, our capacity to extinguish mankind?

We are very complex beings, and we seem to be bifurcated between an outer self and an inner self. In my opinion—underscore "in my opinion"—the innate nature of man is good, basically good. For me, our inner self seems to be in touch with God and communicating with Him regularly. This inner self is likeable, caring, compassionate. The instincts of the inner are right ordered, well ordered. The outer self appears to be dominant, and the outer self seems extraordinarily willing to negotiate those basic fundamental principles which arise from within. The outer self is our sophist to the world. Inner, outer self, each experience some victories, some defeats.

Tension between an inner and outer self is both wearing and worrying. The problem is that this tension does not have to be inner, outer, can be one, should be one. They should be in such close relationship with each other that you can't tell where one leaves off and the other begins. They should be congruent. Our demonstrable actions reflect our inner reality.

Now, this point is made very well by Jonathan Schell, who is writing a series of articles in the *New Yorker* on nuclear arms. This one statement I take from one of those articles: If the inner landscape of the soul does not change, the outer landscape of the world does not change either. And once the choice is made, it must, like every profound moral and spiritual decision, be continually refreshed and renewed. The inner self, notwithstanding its nature, is not static. It needs improvement. The fusion of inner and outer self should result in a whole person fully aware that God's work is truly our own. This awareness should be presaged by a personal view from each of us about the innate nature of man.

Now, I gave you my personal opinion. For centuries, the issue of the innate nature of man has been discussed: Are we good, are we evil, basically? The ancient Chinese philosopher Mencius taught this: Humans are inherently good and fall into evil ways by forgetting or losing their original capacity for goodness.

In direct opposition to that point of view, another Chinese philosopher, Hun Su, taught: Man is by nature evil, and goodness is the result of conscious activity. And then there is the biblical view of human nature: Man was created in the image of God and fell from grace through his own act of rebellion.

Whatever your view about the nature of man, there is no precedent, historical or contemporary, for man to be two people in one. There is no precedent for that. This is a duality which we have contrived for our convenience. We can talk about this and explain our aberrant behavior without saying much more.

As a people with merged, with fused inner and outer selves, we eliminate the distinction between image and reality. We cease projecting shadows where substance is required. That person who is whole has a non-negotiable set of values, a non-negotiable set of principles. Core beliefs, they are advanced boldly. These core beliefs of this whole person include—well, [they include] several things, but I want to just mention two.

The first, justice. Justice is the flagship principle. Justice is the overarching principle. Justice is fairness. Justice is proportionality. Justice is rectification. Justice is equity. Justice.

It was Reinhold Niebuhr who said that justice is the highest ideal of society. A belief in justice is very simple: Everyone is treated fairly by everyone else. There is nothing very complicated about that belief, but the whole person has it.

This entitlement, entitled to be treated fairly by everyone else, this entitlement is so simple because it is right. It is just right that everybody is entitled to be treated as fairly as everybody else, and you need nothing sophisticated, no deep insight, to recognize that basic right.

Justice should be followed by just acts. This is a belief that justice should pervade our personal and our institutional relationships.

Another ingredient, the second one that I will include in this four set of beliefs of this whole person, selflessness. Oh, that is hard. It is very difficult to attain selflessness. Why is it difficult? Well, it is just natural for self-preservation to be paramount for us. But if self-preservation is paramount, you are failing to actualize the spirit of Christ. There is no doubt about that. Self-denial feels very alien on a landscape of acquisitiveness, profits, competition, progress. Self-denial—yes, we ought to have it.

God's work is for the many, not the few. We can deny ourselves some things. If sacrifice is a requirement for the common good, let's sacrifice. That's required of us. It is so much easier to pay lip service to sacrifice than to really do it. Oh, how we like to beat our breasts and say how we are suffering and what we are giving up. But we can sacrifice. God's strengthening of us and our knowledge of God's requirements of us, which were read by Senator Javits from Micah, what does the Lord require of thee, God's strengthening of us and acknowledgment of his requirements of us will help us sacrifice.

To what end has this merger of inner and outer self occurred? What difference does it make that we have this fusion of inner and outer self? Well, if we are whole people, there are some very old words which will be used to define us, words like truth, virtue, honesty. Our political and policy decisions will be released once we are old. Our political and policy decisions will be released, can be released for ethical analysis and hold up wonderful, with a good conscience our only sure reward, with history the final judge of our needs.

Let us go forth and lead the land we love, asking His blessing and His help but knowing that here on earth God's work must truly be our own.

Thank you.

THE SYLVANUS THAYER AWARD

UNSWERVING DEDICATION TO PRINCIPLE

ON OCTOBER 5, 1995, THREE AND A HALF MONTHS BEFORE her death, Barbara Jordan received the Sylvanus Thayer Award presented by the Association of Graduates of the United States Military Academy. West Point describes the award this way:

> [It is presented to] an outstanding citizen of the United States whose service and accomplishments in the national interest exemplify personal devotion to the ideals expressed in the West Point motto, "Duty, Honor, Country." The award is named in honor of Sylvanus Thayer, Class of 1808, the thirty-third graduate of the academy, who nine years later became its fifth superintendent. Serving in this capacity until 1833, Thayer instituted at West Point those principles of academic and military education, based upon the integration of character and knowledge, which have remained an essential element of the Military Academy.[11]

The Sylvanus Thayer Award has been offered continuously since 1958. Some of those previously honored were Generals of the Army Dwight D. Eisenhower, Douglas MacArthur, and Omar N. Bradley; former Presidents Ronald Reagan and George H. W. Bush; Secretaries of State John Foster Dulles, Dean Rusk, Cyrus R. Vance, and George P. Shultz; Supreme Court Chief Justice Warren E. Burger; and a host of other outstanding citizens, such as Reverend Theodore M. Hesburgh, Clare Boothe Luce, Francis Cardinal Spellman, and Billy Graham. Barbara Jordan was in good company.

One line from the "1995 Sylvanus Thayer Award Citation" is worth emphasizing:

> Through the eloquence of her oratory, her relentless pursuit of equal

justice under law, and her unswerving dedication to principle, she has left an indelible imprint upon generations of Americans.

Out of that "unswerving dedication to principle," she addressed those young West Point cadets with these words:

In one hundred and ninety-three years of this institution, our famous warrior sons and daughters have come from West Point. These men and women who helped set your standards have led us in war and in peace. What set them apart from all others?

Is it not the ability and the courage to deny one's self? The ability to remain unswayed by unworthy motives and inconsequential reasons?

Why are you here? I believe for one purpose that transcends all others. To serve your country. You made a decision with monumental consequences when you entered the United States Military Academy.

She concluded:

If the idea of service before self becomes ingrained in you—as West Point will give it every opportunity—you will leave here with the necessary tools to lead our country in the twenty-first century.

You will do so with honor.

The award citation and Barbara Jordan's remarks of acceptance follow. This was her last public address. At a time when our nation is engaged in an armed conflict abroad, her words to those West Point cadets are particularly meaningful.

Jordan receiving the Sylvanus Thayer Award, U.S. Military Academy at
West Point, October 5, 1995. Photo courtesy of Barbara Jordan Archives,
Robert James Terry Library, Texas Southern University, Houston.

1995 SYLVANUS THAYER AWARD CITATION, WEST POINT, OCTOBER 5

EDWARD C. MEYER, GENERAL (RETIRED), CHAIRMAN, ASSOCIATION OF GRADUATES

As a distinguished author, public servant, and educator, Professor Barbara Jordan has rendered a lifetime of outstanding service to the United States and to her fellow citizens. In unusually diverse and multiple fields of endeavor and in positions of extraordinary responsibility, Barbara Jordan, through her accomplishments in the national interest and manner of achievement, has exemplified the ideals of West Point as expressed in its motto, "Duty, Honor, Country."

Barbara Jordan's extraordinary journey from the segregated Houston neighborhood of her childhood to legendary figure on the national stage is replete with firsts. Deciding early in life to be something out of the ordinary, she honed her gift for public speaking in high school and later at Texas Southern University, where she won national recognition in competitive debate and oratory. After graduating magna cum laude, she enrolled in the Boston University School of Law.

Following graduation in 1959, she was admitted to the bar in both Massachusetts and Texas. Choosing to return to her native state, she opened her private practice in Houston. In 1965, Barbara Jordan ran for the Texas Senate and won with a two-to-one majority—the first African American woman ever elected to that body. An astute student of Texas legislative procedure, her performance was so effective that her thirty white male colleagues named her outstanding freshman senator during her first year in office. In 1972, she was elected president pro tem of the senate and, when appointed Texas governor for a day, became the first African American governor in our nation's history.

Barbara Jordan was elected to the United States House of Representatives in 1972 and again was a trailblazer—the first African American woman to be elected from the deep South. During her three terms in office, she served on the Government Operations and Judiciary Committees and was instrumental in the passage of key voting and civil rights legislation.

As a member of the Judiciary Committee, she participated in the nationally televised impeachment proceedings of former President Nixon. In her opening testimony to the committee, she strode boldly into the consciousness of the nation with these now famous words: "My faith in the Constitution is whole. It is complete. It is total. I am not going to sit here and be an idle spectator to the diminution, the subversion, the destruction of the Constitution."

In 1977, Barbara Jordan announced that she would not seek a fourth term in Congress. A year after leaving office, she entered the field of higher education, accepting the Lyndon B. Johnson Public Service Professorship at the LBJ School of Public Affairs, the University of Texas. In 1982, she was selected to hold the Lyndon B. Johnson Centennial Chair in National Policy at the LBJ School of Public Affairs. As an educator, she has become legendary. Her courses are so oversubscribed that attending students are chosen by lottery.

Although no longer in government, she continues to serve our nation—most recently as the chair of the United States Immigration Reform Commission. Barbara Jordan serves as a board member of six major corporations. She is the recipient of more than thirty honorary degrees. She has received numerous national awards, including designation as "Best Living Orator," induction into the National Women's Hall of Fame, and most notably, the Presidential Medal of Freedom.

Throughout her long and dedicated service to our country, both in and out of government, Barbara Jordan has made a lasting contribution to the welfare of others and to the articulation of the ethical foundations of American government. Through the eloquence of her oratory, her relentless pursuit of equal justice under law, and her unswerving dedication to principle, she has left an indelible imprint upon generations of Americans. Accordingly, the Association of Graduates of the United States Military Academy hereby awards the 1995 Sylvanus Thayer Award to Professor Barbara Jordan.

BARBARA JORDAN'S THAYER AWARD ACCEPTANCE

To be chosen to receive the Sylvanus Thayer award is a personal tribute of high and unmatched quality. This single event places me among a group of distinguished Americans you believe best embodies the core principles of West Point. Duty. Honor. Country. My unequivocal delight is enhanced by your presence. Your decision to attend this institution was not a trivial one. You had to discard unnecessary irrelevancies and distracting engagements and commit yourselves to a path designed to add distinction to your country.

I believe I am looking at an audience that includes future Thayer Award winners. By your desire to come to this place, by your admittance through a rigorous screening process, and by your work while here, you have already shown that you are the resource from which leaders will emerge.

I know it must be difficult being a cadet. And I know as you sit here, with part of your attention focused on me and another part focused on the obligations of your cadet life, you are perhaps thinking that I am guilty of great understatement. Of course it is difficult being a cadet!

I know through conversations with some of your predecessors and through anecdotes that filter through the press and other media—some true, some perhaps exaggerated—that yours is an education unlike any other. Demands are placed on you that cause shudders in most of your peers around the nation. It is difficult, as you try to live up to your own standards and those of the school, to consider the very important philosophical context of a West Point education.

But it is important to take the time to examine your purpose and to understand that you are not here simply to get a degree. You could have done that anywhere. You are *not* here just to go through the motions and endure these West Point rites of passage.

Duty. Honor. Country. What a marvelous resonance those words have. Indeed, hallowed words, as Douglas MacArthur called them in 1962. It is not just the sound of their syllables placed together that gives them resonance. It is their historical context. It is the assumptions that undergird those three words.

Duty. Honor. Country. A host of tested and proven values are cast together in those six syllables.

Can you do what is necessary through your service to your country to give those words a meaning that will not only suffice, but challenge and lead others in the twenty-first century?

You must understand those words in order to allow your life to fulfill their meaning in depth and to expand that meaning through the service rendered.

A biographer of the Duke of Marlborough, writing in 1894, said that "in England, the noble, selfless word *duty* has long been the motto of her famous warrior sons."

A noble, selfless word. We should understand duty in the context of a noble, selfless word rather than as simply something that has to be done. Dwight Eisenhower, who preceded me on this stage by thirty-four years, was a student of the concept of duty. "No man can always be right," he wrote. "So the struggle is to do one's best; to keep the brain and conscience clear; never to be swayed by unworthy motives and inconsequential reasons, but to strive to unearth the basic factors involved and then to do one's duty."

In the one hundred and ninety-three years of this institution, our famous warrior sons and daughters have come from West Point. These men and women who helped set your standards have led us in war and in peace. What set them apart from all others?

Is it not the ability and the courage to deny one's self? The

ability to remain unswayed by unworthy motives and inconsequential reasons?

Why are you here? I believe for one purpose that transcends
all others. To serve your country. You made a decision with monumental consequences when you entered the United States Military Academy.

If I were to look each of you in the eyes and ask why you came
to West Point, I think you would agree that not every honest
answer would place service of country at the top of the list. Some
of you have more practical reasons for being here. Perhaps it was
parental pressure. Perhaps it was the realization that you could
not afford this level of education at any other school. Perhaps it
was the desire to become the world's premier engineer.

Nothing is wrong with personal motivation. Nothing is wrong
with understanding the worth of a West Point education. Certainly nothing is wrong with a desire to be the best. The key to
your success at this institution, however, will be your ability to
mature your personal motivation into a selfless motivation. The
rewards for both you and the country will be far greater.

Those of you who accomplish great things in service to your
country will be those who learn the meaning of denial of self.

Those of you who will accomplish great things will achieve the
elevation of character that constitutes honor.

Among the world's great writers at the time of West Point's
founding were William Wordsworth and Samuel Taylor Coleridge. Each wrote about honor in the same context in which we
are considering duty, honor, and country tonight. Coleridge said
that honor implies "a reverence for the invisible and supersen-
sual in our nature." Again, a denial of self. Wordsworth said that
honor "tis the finest sense of justice that the human mind can
frame."

You will be the decision makers of the future. You will literally
hold the lives and fortunes of others within your power. It is my
hope that your circumstances will not include warfare, but they
very well may. If you do not develop honor, if you do not embrace

the finest sense of justice that the human mind can frame, you will not be worthy of the confidence West Point and your country will place in you.

How many times since you first stepped on this campus have you heard words to the effect that the role of the military is changing radically in these post–Cold War years? I hope you do not become numb to the meaning of the changing military role. Instead, take those words as compliments. For if your role were not changing, if you were not willing to change and shape change, then I suggest that you would not be of West Point caliber.

Some things do not change. High ethical values inspirited by your principles. Duty. Honor. Country. They do not change.

Your mission statement should be a constant inspiration to you. "Each graduate shall have the attributes essential to professional growth throughout a career as an officer of the regular Army," it reads in part. Growth means change. Do not fear change. Embrace it as part of your mission.

I am aware that tradition is important here. You are still being taught by some of the methods established by Sylvanus Thayer in the 1820s. Do not mistake adherence to successful tradition for a fear of change. One of your predecessors told me of the standing joke that West Point represents 193 years of tradition unhampered by progress.

If tradition means a steadfast adherence to the highest ethical standards; if tradition means an unfailing dedication to your duty; if tradition means leadership with character; then let this tradition continue for the next 193 years.

If you practice the highest ethical standards, if you are dedicated to your duty, and if you lead with character as Sylvanus Thayer taught, you will then be able to embrace change without fear. Tradition and change are not antithetical. If you look at those you have honored before me, you will see the embodiment of the weaving of tradition and the ability to embrace change.

By enrolling in, and by now I hope embracing, the West Point tradition, you have accepted a lifetime of public service. You will be held—you *should* be held—to higher ethical standards than anyone else. By accepting a lifetime of public service you have also accepted the public trust.

For 193 years, that public trust has been well placed. West Point is where leadership is born. West Point is not just famous names. It is men and women who achieve great things. It is people who built the east–west railroads, people who built the Panama Canal, people who have gone to the Moon.

One hundred and ninety-three years ago we had just begun this grand experiment called democracy. We were not a mature nation. We were just beginning to define our character and find our footing as a country. Here—at West Point—the seeds were planted. The men and women of West Point watered our native soil. We have grown and excelled as a nation in no small part because of the work of your West Point family tree.

Of course, you should not expect that by attending West Point or being graduated from here you will automatically achieve some form of immortality. Not every graduate does. Just as at every great educational institution, West Point has seen its share of graduates who have not lived up to the principles of duty, honor, and country. No system is perfect. After all, we are human. We have weaknesses and fears and misfortune.

There is no magic formula to guarantee success. I can assure you that if you embrace your West Point heritage . . . if you go beyond the dictionary definitions of duty, honor, country and learn their meanings . . . if these words are inculcated into your very souls and are not just everyday chatter . . . you will not need magic formulas.

Your West Point education is only the beginning. But a marvelous beginning. If the idea of service before self becomes ingrained in you—as West Point will give it every opportunity—you will leave here with the necessary tools to lead our country in the twenty-first century.

You will do so with honor.

Thank you, and good luck.

Barbara Jordan, Vernon Jordan, and President Lyndon B. Johnson at a civil rights symposium held at the LBJ Library, December 12, 1972. LBJ Library photo by Frank Wolf, courtesy the Lyndon B. Johnson Presidential Library, Austin.

EPILOGUE

When Max Sherman called to tell me that Barbara was dying and wanted me to speak at this service, I had been reading a story in that morning's *New York Times* about the discovery of forty billion new galaxies deep in the inner sanctum of the universe. Forty billion new galaxies to go with the ten billion we already knew about. As I put the phone down, I thought: it will take an infinite cosmic vista to accommodate a soul this great. The universe had been getting ready for her.

Now, at last, she has an amplifying system equal to that voice. As we gather in her memory, I can imagine the cadences of her eloquence echoing at the speed of light past orbiting planets and pulsars, past black holes and white dwarfs and hundreds of millions of sun-like stars, until the whole cosmic spectrum stretching out to the far fringes of space towards the very origins of time resonates to her presence.

The day after she died, the headline in the *Houston Chronicle* said: "A voice for justice dies." And I thought: Not so. The body dies: "dust to dust and ashes to ashes." But the voice that speaks for justice joins the music of the spheres. What does the universe even know of justice unless informed by a Barbara Jordan? Cock your ear toward the mysterious and invisible matter that shapes the galaxies and sustains their coherence, and you will hear nothing of justice. On matters of meaning and morality, the universe is dumbstruck, the planets silent. Our notions of right and wrong, of how to live together, come from our prophets, not from the planets. It is the human voice that commands justice to roll down "like waters, and righteousness like a mighty stream."

And what a voice this was!

They say that after Theodore Roosevelt was in heaven a few days, he complained to St. Peter that the choir was weak and needed to be reorganized. "All right," said St. Peter, "re-organize it." And Teddy Roosevelt replied: "Well, I'll need 10,000 sopranos, 10,000 altos, and 10,000 tenors."

"And what about the basses?" asked St. Peter.

"Oh," said Teddy Roosevelt, "*I'll* sing bass."

Well, they can all retire in heaven now. Sopranos, altos, tenors—and Teddy, too. There's a new choir in town, and she's a Baptist from the Fifth Ward of Houston.

Barbara was singing the last time we were together. There were two score of us at Liz Carpenter's up on Skyline Drive, belting forth old favorites from the *Broadman and Cokesbury* hymnals. "Standing on the Promises," "Throw Out the Lifeline," "The Old Rugged Cross." And spirituals, too. "Swing Low, Sweet Chariot," "Deep River," "My Lord, What a Morning." Friends have said that her music often eased the smarting wounds of her long battle with multiple sclerosis. But this night some other wellspring opened as she sang one of her favorite blues. Hands on the arms of her electric chariot, that big head tilted back, a mischievous gleam of light in her eyes, she sang: "Nobody knows you when you're down and out. It seems mighty strange without a doubt. But nobody knows you when you're down and out. I mean, when you're down and out."

I recall that moment now, but the Barbara Jordan who appears in my mind's eye is *not* the mature, powerful, accomplished, and celebrated woman whose music filled our circle of fellowship and our hearts that night. No, I see a small child in Houston looking up at a water cooler posted "Whites Only." I see a little girl riding in the back of a bus to a movie she has to enter through a side door to sit in the balcony as prescribed by law. I see a teenager in a segregated high school preparing to go, as expected, to an all-black college. And I see the young collegian leading the Texas Southern debating team and placing first in oratory against all her white opponents but required, even in victory, to sleep in quarters and eat in restaurants marked "For Colored Only." I see a young woman coming back from Boston to open her law practice on the dining room table of her parents' modest brick house at a time that no white firm would hire her. I see her running for office and losing. Running again—and losing. But each time, getting up and coming back without bitterness and rancor, and on her third time, winning. I see her arriving in Austin, a political oddity and outcast, and I see her just six years later, Speaker Pro Tem of the Texas Senate.

How does it happen—when "nobody knows you when you're down and out"? Well, Barbara knew herself. All along the way, with the shadow of Jim Crow falling across every step like an eclipse of the sun, she knew herself. She knew her family, too— her mother, Arlyne, and father, Benjamin, who told her once: "I'll stick with you and go with you as far as you want to go." And Rosemary and Bennie—she knew her sisters and the songs they sang together. And she knew the people of Good Hope Missionary Baptist Church, where reportedly God called often.

She knew her ancestors, too. Not only the bloodlines running back to the sharecroppers and tenant farmers and former slaves and proud Africans, but her political lineage as well.

Socrates was Barbara's kin; with him she believed you cannot have a healthy state when "you have one half the world triumphing and the other plunged in grief." And *Plato* was her kin, exhorting young people, as she did, to "take part in the great combat, which is the contest of life."

Montesquieu was her kin, who said the state of nature bestows on us an equality that society then robs from us, and we recover it "only by the protection of the laws." With him, she would hold that "a government is like everything else; to preserve it, we must love it."

Edmund Burke was her kin, who held that "all persons possessing any portion of power ought to be strongly and awfully impressed with the idea that they act in trust; and that they are to account for their conduct in that trust to the one great Master, Author, and Founder of society."

And *Lincoln*—Lincoln was surely Barbara's kin, who said, "We will make converts day by day. And unless truth be a mockery and justice a hollow lie, we will be in the majority after a while...." Who also said: "The battle of freedom is to be fought out on principle."

Dead white males—from Greece, France, England, and Illinois. And a black woman from Houston. Kin. Not by blood. Not through the color of skin. Not from place of birth or tribe of origin. Not by station, rank, or office. No, kinship in the universal republic is forged from the love of a vision of truth, *passion* for the spirit of liberty, and the *conviction* that justice is so embedded in the social fabric, it cannot long be denied if a people are to prosper.

Now what made Barbara so effective is the way she brought those ideas to down-home politics. True, she was an extraordinary speaker. It was said of the famous Methodist preacher George Whitfield, "He could make men laugh or cry by pronouncing the single word 'Mesopotamia.'" Barbara could do it with the word "Constitution." But her ambitions were not for a few lines of immortality in *Bartlett's Book of Quotations:* nor was she content to capture your heart. She wanted your vote.

No nonsense.

Over in Houston, she began in politics licking stamps and knocking on doors; they still talk about the time she organized the city's first black precinct drive for Kennedy and Johnson in 1960. Here in Austin, almost half the bills she submitted for consideration were enacted into law. In a legislature that was practically an oligarchy, she made things happen for laundry workers, domestic helpers, and farm laborers.

And up in Washington, for only three terms, she so mastered the process and details of procedure that not even the craftiest patriarchs of Congress could outfox her. Her 1975 campaign to hold Texas accountable to the Voting Rights Act was a triumph over entrenched and powerful opponents. A journalist colleague of mine said she was "as cozy as a pile driver, but considerably more impressive." But in her study of the art of politics, she had clearly listened to the counsel of the experienced, which holds that "as with sailing, so with politics; make your cloth too taut, and your ship will dip and keel, but slacken off and trim your sails, and things head off again."

Maybe she got that from her political godfathers, Franklin Roosevelt and Lyndon Johnson. Roosevelt was a hero to her family because her family owed to his election the little brick house that her grandfather was able to buy in Houston with help from the Home Finance Corporation. And LBJ showed her how to maneuver among movers and shakers without being moved and shaken from her principles. Like both of them, she understood that America's development owed much of its story to the affirmative action of government. From the common purse, throughout our history, had poured money for just about every improvement you could name—canals, dams, roads, forts, river channels, mining and fishing rights, and even orange groves. So she argued, as both Roosevelt and Johnson had argued, that the fruits of democracy belonged on the table of the simplest home no less than in the banquet hall of the grandest mansion.

But she was no creature of government. She went, she served, and she came home. After six years in office, she voluntarily imposed term limits upon her career in Congress, before there was a national movement to make them mandatory. Woodrow Wilson had said, "Things get very lonely in Washington. The real voice of the great people of America sometimes sounds faint and distant in that strange city." Not for Barbara Jordan. She heard the voice of the people, and she gave the people a voice.

No wonder they held her in respect approaching reverence. After her death, people who had never met her poured out their personal eulogies. I came upon one last Friday in a letter to the *Los Angeles Times*. It was signed by a twenty-four-year-old immigrant from Chile named Fabio Escobar. Here's what he said: "I did not grow up in the United States. I do not remember the Watergate hearings or Jordan's keynote address at the 1976 Democratic Convention. I only learned of her career while studying philosophy and political science at Cal State a few years ago. I never met her except through the books and tapes of her speeches. But I know Barbara Jordan's accomplishments extend far beyond the narrow scope of the political realm. She spoke for millions of individuals who yearned for leaders who would commit themselves to a core set of issues grounded not in polls, but in the solid footing of raw, personal conviction. No American politician of recent times has done that better than she did. She stood on conviction and fought for what she believed was right. This is the noblest and most difficult task a person can undertake, and she did it with exceptional quality." This, from a young man whose native language was Spanish.

To people like Fabio Escobar, Barbara Jordan was an inspiration; to others, a hero; to the lucky, a friend. To me, she was all these things, and something more. In 1987, she became my muse.

That summer was the two hundredth anniversary of the Constitutional Convention in Philadelphia, where remarkable minds had talked the United States into being. So I made the Constitution, in 1987, my "beat" on PBS.

Some of the programs my colleagues and I produced were *unabashedly celebratory*. I still marvel that any group of fifty-six prickly men, meeting in the breathless heat of an urban summer, could have agreed on anything, let alone a firm and lasting foundation for a new kind of nation no one had ever seen before. But some of our programs that summer were much less hopeful and much less proud—because even as in 1987 we were celebrating the making of our Constitution, we were also watching its attempted *undoing*, as the Iran-Contra scandal revealed yet one more conspiracy to subvert the Constitution by those who had sworn to uphold it.

Reporting on the Iran-Contra scandal that summer, I took heart in recalling Barbara's stirring words during the Watergate hearings scarcely a decade earlier. There, she had famously declared her whole and total faith in the Constitution despite having been excluded from it. The Convention of 1787 had decided people like her were only 60 percent a person, which is how slaves and others were to be enumerated for the purposes of representation. But the truth is, Barbara Jordan would have fit right in with any of the 100 percent white men in that hall, two hundred years ago, in her understanding of justice.

George Mason had asked: "Shall any man be above Justice?"

Edmund Randolph had declared: "Guilt wherever found ought to be punished."

And Gouveneur Morris had said: "The Magistrate is not the King. The people are the King."

And what might Barbara Jordan have said?

This, perhaps: "If the society today allows wrongs to go unchallenged, the impression is created that those wrongs have the approval of the majority."

Certainly this: "Justice of the right is always to take precedence over might."

The founders would have been lucky to have had her in that Constitutional Convention. And if she had been present, it would have taken far less time for Barbara Jordan to be recognized as a whole person in the sight of the law, or for this country to fulfill its promise.

As it is, the good fortune has been yours and mine. Just when we despaired of finding a hero, she showed up, to give the sign of democracy.

Do you know what the odds of this happening had to be? That

in a universe existing billions of years, with fifty billion galaxies and more, on a planet of modest size, circling an ordinary sun in an unexceptional galaxy, that you and I would have arrived in the same time zone as Barbara Jordan, at such a moment of serendipity to be touched by this one woman's life, to encounter her spirit and her faith?

This is no small thing. This is grace.

NOTES

1. Whenever possible I use the words of Barbara Jordan's students. The factual biography is from the student-organized Seventh Annual Barbara Jordan National Forum on Public Policy: Rejuvenating Ethics, Commitment & Responsibility in Today's America, held at the Lyndon B. Johnson School of Public Affairs at the University of Texas at Austin in 2003. The student comments that follow were recorded by the Lyndon B. Johnson Presidential Library and Museum, Austin.

2. The proposed new area for "Texas Heroes" was never implemented. Col. Fannin is still buried at Goliad. Harry Bradley, Superintendent, Texas State Cemetery, personal communication, March 16, 2006.

3. Sharpstown Stock-Fraud Scandal, http://www.tsha.utexas.edu/handbook/online/articles/TT/mk+2.html, (accessed March 16, 2006).

4. Mary Beth Rogers, *Barbara Jordan: American Hero* (New York: Bantam Books, 1998), pp. 157–165.

5. Ibid., pp. 205–219.

6. Most of the information in this paragraph comes from "The Handbook of Texas Online, TSHA Online," Texas Legislature, http://www.tsha.utexas.edu/handbook/online/articles/SS/mqs1.html, (accessed March 16, 2006).

7. Press release, the White House, Office of the Press Secretary, December 14, 1993.

8. Testimony of Susan Martin, Executive Director, U.S. Commission on Immigration Reform, before the U.S. Senate Committee on the Judiciary, Subcommittee on Immigration, February 6, 1996.

9. Testimony of Barbara Jordan, Chair, U.S. Commission on Immigration Reform, Before the U.S. House of Representatives Committee on Ways and Means, Subcommittee on Human Resources, August 9, 1994.

10. Robert A. Caro, *The Years of Lyndon Johnson: Master of the Senate* (New York: Knopf, 2002), p. 523.

11. The Sylvanus Thayer Award, http://www.virtualwp.org/channel_closeup_experience_thayer_award.htm, (accessed March 16, 2006).

Jordan being sworn in as "Governor for a Day," the first African American to be so honored, June 10, 1972. Photo courtesy of Barbara Jordan Archives, Robert James Terry Library, Texas Southern University, Houston (hereafter Jordan Archives, TSU).

Jordan speaking at her "Governor for a Day" ceremony, June 10, 1972. Photo courtesy of Archives Division, Texas State Library, Austin.

Jordan with Lyndon Johnson at the Shamrock Hotel in Houston, announcing her candidacy for U.S. Congress, 1973. Photo courtesy of Jordan Archives, TSU.

Freshman congresswoman Barbara Jordan with President Lyndon Johnson.
Photo courtesy of Jordan Archives, TSU.

Jordan and Andrew Young with John Doar. Photo courtesy of Jordan Archives, TSU.

Jordan with member of Girls' Nation on the steps of the Capitol.
Photo courtesy of Jordan Archives, TSU.

The Democratic congressional delegation from Texas. To Jordan's left is Senator Lloyd Bentsen. Photo courtesy of Jordan Archives, TSU.

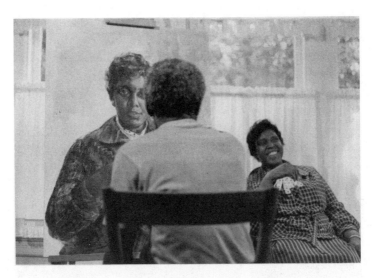

Jordan smiling while the artist, Edsel M. Cramer, paints her official portrait. Photo courtesy of Jordan Archives, TSU.

With President Gerald R. Ford at the signing of the Voting Rights Act of 1975, August 6, 1975. Photo courtesy of Archives Division, Texas State Library, Austin.

Speaking at the Lyndon B. Johnson Presidential Library in 1975.
Photo courtesy of the LBJ School of Public Affairs.

Delivering her keynote address at the Democratic National Convention, July 12,
1976. Behind Jordan is the chairman of the Democratic National Committee,
Robert Strauss. Photo courtesy of Jordan Archives, TSU.

Jordan loved to sing. Here she is, playing the guitar, with a group of friends in 1971.
Photo courtesy of Max Sherman.

Along with Bernard Rapoport, Jordan enjoys a great play at a University of Texas women's basketball game. Photo courtesy of Jordan Archives, TSU.

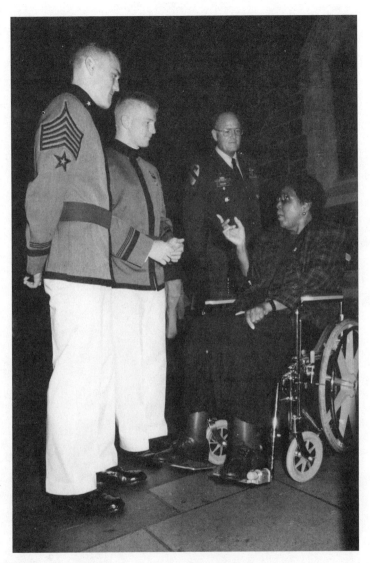

Jordan with cadets from the U.S. Military Academy at West Point shortly after being awarded the Sylvanus Thayer Award, October 5, 1995. Photo courtesy of Jordan Archives, TSU.

Jordan with Nobel laureate and former president of South Africa Nelson Mandela. Photo courtesy of Jordan Archives, TSU.

Jordan with
children at a
day care center
in Wenyenge,
eastern Transvaal,
South Africa, in
the summer of
1991. Photograph
from the Kaiser
Family Foundation,
courtesy of the
LBJ School of
Public Affairs.

Jordan with
students during
class at the LBJ
School, 1990.
Photo courtesy of
the LBJ School of
Public Affairs.

Jordan celebrating her fifty-fourth birthday with a cake presented to her in class by her students. Photo by María de la Luz Martínez, courtesy of the LBJ School of Public Affairs.

The University of Texas Students' Memorial March for Barbara Jordan, January 19, 1996. UT President Robert Berdahl addresses a group in front of the Lyndon B. Johnson Presidential Library. Photo by María de la Luz Martínez, courtesy of the LBJ School of Public Affairs.